# Learning
# Disabilities

# OTHER BOOKS OF RELATED INTEREST

# Learning Disabilities

Henny H. Kim, *Book Editor*

Daniel Leone, *President*
Bonnie Szumski, *Publisher*
Scott Barbour, *Managing Editor*
Brenda Stalcup, *Series Editor*

## Contemporary Issues
### Companion

GREENHAVEN
PRESS ®

THOMSON
™
GALE

San Diego • Detroit • New York • San Francisco • Cleveland
New Haven, Conn. • Waterville, Maine • London • Munich

**LIBRARY OF CONGRESS CATALOGING-IN-PUBLICATION DATA**

Learning Disabilities / Henny H. Kim, book editor.
   p. cm. — (Contemporary issues companion)
   Includes bibliographical references and index.
   ISBN 0-7377-1622-3 (pbk. : alk. paper) —
   ISBN 0-7377-1621-5 (lib. bdg. : alk. paper)
   1. Learning disabilities. 2. Learning disabled children—Education. I. Kim, Henny
H., 1968– . II. Series.
LC4704.L394 2004
371.92'6—dc21
                       4653                                2003054010

Printed in the United States of America

# CONTENTS

**Chapter 4: People with Learning Disabilities: Personal Narratives**

# FOREWORD

In the news, on the streets, and in neighborhoods, individuals are confronted with a variety of social problems. Such problems may affect people directly: A young woman may struggle with depression, suspect a friend of having bulimia, or watch a loved one battle cancer. And even the issues that do not directly affect her private life—such as religious cults, domestic violence, or legalized gambling—still impact the larger society in which she lives. Discovering and analyzing the complexities of issues that encompass communal and societal realms as well as the world of personal experience is a valuable educational goal in the modern world.

Effectively addressing social problems requires familiarity with a constantly changing stream of data. Becoming well informed about today's controversies is an intricate process that often involves reading myriad primary and secondary sources, analyzing political debates, weighing various experts' opinions—even listening to firsthand accounts of those directly affected by the issue. For students and general observers, this can be a daunting task because of the sheer volume of information available in books, periodicals, on the evening news, and on the Internet. Researching the consequences of legalized gambling, for example, might entail sifting through congressional testimony on gambling's societal effects, examining private studies on Indian gaming, perusing numerous websites devoted to Internet betting, and reading essays written by lottery winners as well as interviews with recovering compulsive gamblers. Obtaining valuable information can be time-consuming—since it often requires researchers to pore over numerous documents and commentaries before discovering a source relevant to their particular investigation.

Greenhaven's Contemporary Issues Companion series seeks to assist this process of research by providing readers with useful and pertinent information about today's complex issues. Each volume in this anthology series focuses on a topic of current interest, presenting informative and thought-provoking selections written from a wide variety of viewpoints. The readings selected by the editors include such diverse sources as personal accounts and case studies, pertinent factual and statistical articles, and relevant commentaries and overviews. This diversity of sources and views, found in every Contemporary Issues Companion, offers readers a broad perspective in one convenient volume.

In addition, each title in the Contemporary Issues Companion series is designed especially for young adults. The selections included in every volume are chosen for their accessibility and are expertly edited in consideration of both the reading and comprehension levels of the audience. The structure of the anthologies also enhances accessibility. An introductory essay places each issue in context and provides helpful facts such as historical background or current statistics and legislation that pertain to the topic. The chapters that follow organize the material and focus on specific aspects of the book's topic. Every essay is introduced by a brief summary of its main points and biographical information about the author. These summaries aid in comprehension and can also serve to direct readers to material of immediate interest and need. Finally, a comprehensive index allows readers to efficiently scan and locate content.

The Contemporary Issues Companion series is an ideal launching point for research on a particular topic. Each anthology in the series is composed of readings taken from an extensive gamut of resources, including periodicals, newspapers, books, government documents, the publications of private and public organizations, and Internet websites. In these volumes, readers will find factual support suitable for use in reports, debates, speeches, and research papers. The anthologies also facilitate further research, featuring a book and periodical bibliography and a list of organizations to contact for additional information.

A perfect resource for both students and the general reader, Greenhaven's Contemporary Issues Companion series is sure to be a valued source of current, readable information on social problems that interest young adults. It is the editors' hope that readers will find the Contemporary Issues Companion series useful as a starting point to formulate their own opinions about and answers to the complex issues of the present day.

# INTRODUCTION

School presents a variety of challenges for most children; it takes time and effort to successfully master even basic skills such as reading or writing. But for children who have learning disabilities, these challenges can be magnified a hundredfold. Susan, for example, "hated reading and math because none of the letters, numbers or '+' and '–' signs made any sense," education authority and pediatrician Mel Levine writes. Students like Susan, who have learning disabilities that hinder their comprehension of certain types of material, may be overwhelmed by the conventional educational system. Routine assignments can seem like insurmountable obstacles to these students, causing them to become frustrated with school and embarrassed about their academic performance. They may be ridiculed by their peers, and their teachers may grow exasperated with their seeming inability to learn. According to Levine, Susan received a grim assessment: "She'd been told—and was convinced—that she was retarded."

Actually, Susan was quite intelligent, but her learning disability made it nearly impossible for her to demonstrate her intelligence in a standard school setting. The National Institute of Mental Health (NIMH) defines a learning disability as "a disorder that affects people's ability to either interpret what they see and hear or to link information from different parts of the brain." The term "learning disability" does not pertain to "children who have learning problems which are primarily the result of visual, hearing, or motor handicaps, [or] of mental retardation," according to the Education of the Handicapped Act of 1975. Instead, it applies to children who possess the intellectual capacity to succeed academically but who have difficulty acquiring the technical skills. Although experts are still uncertain as to the exact cause of learning disabilities, many scientists and educators now believe that they are neurological in origin—that a "glitch" in the brain's neural pathways affects how people with learning disabilities process information. Moreover, research has shown that some learning disabilities appear to be hereditary and therefore may have a genetic basis.

Some common learning disabilities include dyslexia (difficulty with language processing, which affects reading, writing, and spelling), dyscalculia (difficulty with math skills), and dysgraphia (difficulty with writing). Closely related is attention deficit hyperactivity disorder (ADHD), which causes extreme restlessness, distractibility, and impulsiveness. Some experts classify ADHD as a learning disability, while others consider it a behavioral disorder that adversely affects learning. It is not uncommon for individuals with ADHD to also have at least one learning disability, such as dyslexia.

Learning disabilities are often called "hidden handicaps" because unlike many physical disabilities, they are not immediately obvious to observers. This aspect can make learning disabilities very difficult to identify and diagnose. However, extensive research in the field has uncovered typical characteristics of learning disabilities, including reversing letters and numbers, frequent confusion about directions and time, difficulty following instructions, short attention span, and impetuous or inappropriate behavior. Signs of learning disabilities may be evident from infancy or early childhood but typically go unnoticed during that stage of development. As educator Sally L. Smith explains, "Especially with a first child, parents may not know when to expect vocalizing, playing with sounds, and learning to speak." Hence, learning disabilities are usually not detected until after the child begins school, when teachers and/or parents grow concerned over the child's slow progress.

A surprisingly high number of people—from all economic and social levels—have learning disabilities. According to NIMH, about 4 million children in the United States have learning disabilities, of which 20 percent have attention disorders. The U.S. Department of Education reports that during the first three years of school, more than one in six children will show signs of mild learning disabilities, including problems with reading. Unfortunately, because these "hidden handicaps" were not well understood in the past, an untold number of students with learning disabilities struggled through their entire school career without receiving proper diagnosis or treatment. Even today, with the vast strides that have been made in the diagnosis of learning disabilities, experts still express concern that many children are being overlooked.

When individuals with learning disabilities reach adulthood without a correct diagnosis, they continue to face disadvantages in the workplace and community. For example, adults with undiagnosed dyslexia may be functionally illiterate—unable to read and understand an employee handbook, an insurance policy, or a lease agreement. Told in school that they were "just stupid," these adults frequently suffer from low self-esteem. Many undiagnosed adults compensate for their sense of inadequacy by trying to hide their educational deficiencies, and they dread the possibility that their secret will be revealed. However, as public awareness about learning disabilities steadily increases, more and more of these adults are realizing the truth about their problems and are finally receiving treatment. With the proper educational guidance, they can learn to cope with their lifelong condition and achieve as much professional and personal success as those who do not have learning disabilities.

Despite such success stories among adults, early diagnosis and intervention is always preferable; the earlier the learning disability is caught, the more likely a child is to develop effective coping methods and alternative learning techniques. Moreover, the longer diagnosis is delayed, the greater the chance that the child will develop a negative self-image, which Levine argues can be worse for a child's healthy mental development than the learning disability itself. An early diagnosis also enables a child to benefit from specific programs intended to aid students with learning disabilities. The Individuals with Disabilities Education Act (IDEA) provides legal protection and educational support for all students with disabilities, including those who have learning disabilities. IDEA mandates that qualified students receive "a team-approved individualized education program" designed to meet "the student's specific learning needs." In addition, the use of technological devices can open new doors for students with learning disabilities. For example, students who have severe dyslexia can listen to textbooks recorded on cassette tapes, and they can compose essays with the assistance of computer programs that recognize oral dictation and convert speech into typed text.

Advances in diagnosis and treatment have given people with learning disabilities more options for building a successful life than ever before. The fact that learning disabilities can be overcome is especially evidenced by the list of famous people who have publicly discussed their own experiences with learning disabilities, including Tom Cruise, Jay Leno, Whoopi Goldberg, and Cher. The growing perception that learning disabilities are widely spread and have afflicted some of the most successful people in the world has done much to lessen the stigma associated with being learning disabled. As actor Henry Winkler declares confidently, "I'm not lazy. I'm not stupid. I'm dyslexic."

Clearly, the recent influx of accurate information about dyslexia and similar disorders has had a positive effect on society's attitude toward people who have learning disabilities. The goal of *Learning Disabilities: Contemporary Issues Companion* is to contribute to this trend by providing a comprehensive overview of the historical, educational, and societal aspects of the different types of learning disabilities. The selections included in this anthology cover a variety of topics, from symptoms and causes to educational approaches and other strategies for achieving success. The final chapter explores the emotional and social impact of learning disabilities through the personal stories of those individuals who, by relating their own struggles and achievements, offer hope to others that learning disabilities can indeed be overcome.

# CHAPTER 1

# LEARNING DISABILITIES: AN OVERVIEW

# COMMON TYPES OF LEARNING DISABILITIES

Jean Cheng Gorman

Jean Cheng Gorman is a psychologist whose research focuses on children's emotional health and learning disabilities; her experience includes teaching in urban and suburban elementary schools. In the following selection from her book *Emotional Disorders and Learning Disabilities in the Elementary Classroom: Interactions and Interventions*, Cheng Gorman presents a survey of the various learning disabilities that appear most frequently in elementary school students. Common learning disabilities, she explains, include those that affect reading, speech, writing, and mathematics. Furthermore, according to Cheng Gorman, other factors that can affect children's schoolwork—such as attention deficit hyperactivity disorder, memory problems, and difficulties in organizing information—are increasingly being recognized by researchers and educators as learning disabilities.

The term *learning disabilities* is a broad term that has been used to encompass problems with language, mathematics, and writing; visual and perceptual problems; and attention or behavior problems. But just what constitutes a learning disability? Some researchers focus on identifying distinct neuropsychological profiles, attempting to find a very scientific or medical definition. Others . . . suggest that the term is inappropriate and inadequate for describing the learning processes of students, because it fails to take into account the "whole child" in an authentic context.

Most educators define learning disabilities according to federal law. The U.S. Office of Education and Public Law 101-476 (Individuals with Disabilities Education Act) defines "specific learning disabilities" as

> a disorder in one or more of the basic psychological processes involved in understanding or in using language, spoken or written, which may manifest itself in imperfect ability to listen, think, speak, read, write, spell, or to do mathematical calculations. The term includes such conditions as perceptual handi-

caps, brain injury, minimal brain dysfunction, dyslexia, and developmental aphasia. The term does not include children who have learning disabilities which are primarily the result of visual, hearing or motor handicaps, or mental retardation, or emotional disturbance, or of environmental, cultural, or economic disadvantage. (U.S. Office of Education, 1977, p. 65083)

Although debate over operationalizing this definition continues, a significant discrepancy between achievement and intellectual ability (as measured by performance on achievement and intelligence tests) is used by many states to identify a student as learning disabled. Some consider at least 2 standard deviations between intellectual ability and academic functioning to be significant. This means that a child whose IQ is 100 (average) would need to score below the 9th percentile for his or her age on diagnostic tests in order to be diagnosed with a learning disability. Most children with learning disabilities have average intelligence but achieve far below what is expected for their age and intelligence. True learning disabilities are thought to be lifelong disorders.

This selection presents a brief overview of learning disorders that may be encountered in the classroom. It is certainly not an exhaustive presentation of learning disabilities, and other works . . . present more in-depth information. Although this selection describes discrete areas of learning disabilities, it is important to bear in mind that many children may have elements of several areas of difficulty that do not fall neatly into the categories featured here. At the same time, several learning problems can stem from a global learning disability. . . .

## Reading Disabilities

Reading disabilities are likely what comes to mind when you think of learning disabilities. Problems with reading can involve many areas, including word recognition and comprehension, oral reading fluency, and reading comprehension. Within each of these areas, numerous skills are needed to successfully read. For example, comprehending a passage involves noting important details, identifying the main idea, tracking a sequence of events or steps, drawing inferences and conclusions, organizing ideas, and applying what is read. Students may have difficulty in any of these higher-order skill areas, although their basic reading skills are intact.

The term *dyslexia* has often been used to refer to reading disabilities, and is a familiar term for many people. Some have overused it to describe all problems with reading and writing or have misunderstood it to be a problem with letter reversals (e.g., writing a "b" instead of a "d"). Others believe the term is obsolete and does not reflect more holistic concepts in language. Still others say that dyslexia is a highly specific disability, partly genetic, likely based in neurological (brain) abnormalities, and does not apply to all children with language-based learning problems.

Despite the controversy, as a type of reading disability, dyslexia is well researched and, relative to other learning disability subtypes, well understood. The core problem area is in phonological processing. There are a total of 44 phonemes in the English language. Different combinations of these small sound units make up words. For example, "kuh," "aah," and "tuh" can be combined to form the word *cat*. A child with dyslexia may have trouble distinguishing between phonemes when they are put together. Alternatively, a child may struggle to combine phonemes into words when writing. Reading becomes a chore because of difficulty identifying the sound units that make up the words. Spelling and writing are challenging for the same reason. Decoding exercises and identifying the number of syllables in a word are exceptionally difficult for children with dyslexia.

## Dyslexia's Difficulties

Neuroscience research raises the possibility that people with dyslexia also have an underlying processing speed deficit in addition to their phonological difficulties. It may be that people with dyslexia process sounds more slowly than average, making it difficult to distinguish phonemes. This provides additional explanation for why people with dyslexia have problems with reading and spoken language, which are commonly very rapid activities.

Children who are dyslexic may not have problems with speech, but may struggle with interpreting what they hear. For instance, because of their phonological processing problems, they may not be able to tell the word *pat* from *bat*. As a result, children with dyslexia may be viewed as "normal" with the exception of being a "poor reader," a "bad listener," or "inattentive." These children may also be attributed with emotional problems, such as "lack of motivation," because their language processing difficulties may not be obvious. As a result, it is possible for a student with significant dyslexia to be undiagnosed until late in elementary school or even beyond. . . . In the early school years, "subjects" are based on acquiring learning skills such as reading. In the upper grades, "subjects" become more content-focused (e.g., history or science lessons), and the ability to read is taken for granted. Consequently, early identification of dyslexia is particularly important, since adequate reading skills are the basis for all other learning. . . .

## Struggles with Communication

Other children struggle not only with reading but in multiple areas of communication. Oral language problems can exist in syntax (the way words are put together to form phrases), semantics (the meanings of words), morphology (word formation), phonology (speech sounds), articulation (producing sounds), and pragmatics (the relationship between words and their users). Communication involves both receptive and expressive language skills. In essence, "receptive language" refers to receiving communication, whereas "expressive language" refers to producing language. Children with receptive language disorders may have problems comprehending single words or may struggle to understand when words are strung together in sentences. They may understand only a part of what is said and respond to that part, or may be entirely confused by what they perceive to be a jumble of words. In a sense, children with significant receptive language problems experience the world in ways similar to someone in a foreign country. Although the sounds of the foreign language can be heard and perhaps even reproduced, the conversations seem meaningless. Children with receptive language problems often also have some difficulties with expressive language.

In contrast, children with expressive language problems can understand what is said to them but may communicate with gestures and in other nonverbal ways, because they have difficulty producing intelligible speech. This is different from speech disorders, such as stuttering and articulation problems, that also interfere with learning but are generally not considered to be a type of learning disability. Rather, expressive language problems can be so significant that a child's speech is meaningless. Usually, expressive language problems are less obvious. For example, 9-year-old Gwen seemed to have a limited vocabulary because she constantly used the word *thing*, and because she tended to describe an object rather than name it (e.g., "that thing you write with" instead of "pencil"). In actuality, she probably had dysnomia, or a deficit in recalling specific words. This deficit was responsible for another student spending over an hour to write five sentences.

Severe receptive or expressive language problems rarely go unnoticed, and generally, such children are referred for a psychoeducational evaluation early on. Often, a child may be overly quiet, for example, or may be described by parents as slow to speak. It is certainly possible, however, for children with milder difficulties to be undiagnosed and to have their problems attributed to other reasons, such as being "shy" or "in their own world." It is also highly possible that the deficits are in both receptive and expressive areas, resulting in a more diffuse presentation that is harder to identify.

## Writing Disorders

Children can have difficulty in many written-language skills, which include handwriting, spelling, punctuation, capitalization, and composition. Perhaps the most common disorder of written expression is a deficiency in spelling. Spelling problems may be a sign of dyslexia and may reflect an underlying problem with phonological processing. Specifically, if a child cannot identify the sound units that make up a word, she or he probably will not be able to accurately combine letters to form the word. However, spelling problems may also be separate from dyslexia and indicate problems in areas other than phonological processing. For example, a child may have difficulty visualizing a word or may struggle when retrieving the word from memory without other contextual or visual cues.

The other common writing disorder is in handwriting. A child with almost illegible handwriting should not be dismissed as "messy" or "careless," but should be evaluated for an underlying learning disability. Handwriting difficulties are considered to be a deficit in written expression and may also be part of a larger nonverbal learning disability. Very poor handwriting may be due to visual-motor deficits, problems with visual perception, fine-motor coordination problems, and/or compromised spatial abilities. The term *dysgraphia* is typically reserved for severe handwriting problems. Although proper penmanship might seem archaic, dysgraphia and even more minor handwriting disorders have significant repercussions in later learning. For example, because of his terrible handwriting, 10-year-old Michael tended to avoid all language arts assignments, even electing not to do tasks he could easily accomplish because it was too tiring to try to write legibly. Children who are unable to write letters of the same size and to maintain an even line will likely have trouble doing math problems that require accurate placement of digits in columns (e.g., borrowing).

## Math Disabilities

Problems with mathematics may stem from a variety of deficits. Careful assessment must determine if the deficiencies truly reside in mathematics, or if they are more reflective of problems of spatial arrangement, attention and concentration, or even reading comprehension. For example, a student who is consistently unable to do word problems may have intact calculation skills but may not be able to read well enough to comprehend the mathematical operation being required. True math disabilities involve problems with math concepts and skills, including computation, problem solving, geometry, mental calculations, estimation, probability, statistics, decimals, measurement, and fractions.

Some use the term *dyscalculia* to refer to a primary disability in learning computation and math concepts. These skill areas include one-to-one correspondence, part-to-whole relationships (e.g., fractions), place value, as well as basic skills such as subtraction and multiplication. Problems with core math skills may be hard to detect, because students with dyscalculia may try to get around their difficulties by relying on counting for computing basic facts, rather than on recall, which can hinder math achievement significantly. Because of their difficulties comprehending the concepts behind the operations, children with dyscalculia may struggle to learn math despite frequent drills and instruction. . . .

## Nonverbal Learning Disabilities

Math disabilities may appear as a circumscribed problem area or may be part of a broader neurologically based condition. For example, developmental Gerstmann syndrome, which includes a constellation of dysgraphia, dyscalculia, and neurological soft-signs (subtle physical abnormalities), is considered a nonverbal learning disorder.

Identification of a nonverbal learning disability may be more difficult than a language-based disability, because it is less well understood. Characteristics of a nonverbal learning disability include tactile-perceptual deficits; psychomotor coordination problems; visual, spatial, and organizational difficulties; problems adapting to novel and complex situations; poor mathematics abilities; and problems in social perception and judgment. . . .

## Other Learning Problems

Other deficits can also affect achievement and are increasingly considered to be learning disabilities. Although these are not formally recognized by schools as necessitating special services, it is helpful to be aware of the growing support for identification of disorders in executive functioning, memory, and self-regulation.

The term *executive functioning* refers to higher-order processes such as planning ahead and organizing information. These functions affect a variety of experiences, making it difficult to pinpoint a learning disability. An example of higher-order problems is difficulty in concept formation. As a result, the child may not be able to generalize from one learning situation to another. It is as if the child has to relearn the concept for every assignment or application. For instance, Stephanie's fourth-grade teacher constantly complained that she seemed to understand what she was teaching one day, then forgot it the next.

Other executive functions include selective attention (e.g., being able to screen out stimuli and focus only on something specific) and inhibitory control (e.g., holding back one's urges). Attention deficit hyperactivity disorder (ADHD) is considered by most educators as more of a behavioral disorder than a learning disorder. . . . However, new research suggests that children with ADHD have fundamental deficits in regulating their internal arousal and attention, as well as impulse control and activity level. These deficits in executive functioning imply that ADHD is related to the fundamental processes of learning, not just to behavior. Interestingly, approximately one fourth of all children with ADHD will also have at least one type of additional learning disability in math, reading, or spelling, further suggesting a need for reconceptualization.

Memory is complex. Remembering something requires noticing it, focusing on it, registering it, storing the information in some meaningful way, and recalling it. Problems with any of these skills result in great difficulties acquiring new information and retrieving previously learned information. Children with fundamental deficits in memory often experience a vicious cycle of learning problems that exists across subject matter. For example, sixth-grader Jin struggled in almost all academic subjects, leading her teachers to believe she was simply a below-average student. However, her worst subject was clearly social studies, because she had a terrible time memorizing all the names, dates, and places. Children with memory deficits may also be seen as having problems in attention or concentration, when in actuality the deficits are more serious.

The concept of self-regulation is fairly new and refers to the ability to monitor one's internal processes and adjust them accordingly to meet situational demands. For example, after seeing a frightening movie, you use various ways to calm yourself down so you can have a pleasant conversation with your friend, rather than feel hypervigilant and suspicious of everything around you in the restaurant. Children with disorders of self-regulation may have difficulty being aware of their heightened arousal and may not be able to shift their internal activity level to adjust to a new situation. For example, a child with poor self-regulatory abilities may not be able to make the transition from gym class to silent reading without significant external prompting and structure (e.g., constant reminders to "calm down"). . . . Cognitive self-regulation, such as being able to set goals, monitor one's progress, and adjust effort accordingly, is also a necessary part of learning. Not being able to "talk oneself through" a difficult task makes problem solving more difficult and learning more arduous.

There is also growing recognition that social, emotional, and behavioral problems typically considered to be childhood psychological or emotion disorders have a strong impact on school achievement and learning.

# Dyslexia: A Complex Learning Style

Cynthia M. Stowe

Dyslexia is one of the best-known learning disabilities. But although many people are familiar with the term *dyslexia*, according to Cynthia M. Stowe, most are unaware of its diverse forms. Dyslexia can be confusing because it does not fit a standard profile, Stowe relates; instead, it manifests in different ways in affected individuals, adversely impacting reading, writing, spelling, and/or handwriting skills. The dyslexic learning style is also associated with specific intellectual strengths, she observes, as evidenced by numerous famous people—among them Albert Einstein and Leonardo da Vinci—who are believed to have had dyslexia yet who achieved great success as adults. Stowe is a consulting psychologist at the Eagle Mountain School in Greenfield, Massachusetts, an independent day school for children with learning disabilities. Her books include children's novels and practical instruction books, as well as *How to Reach and Teach Children and Teens with Dyslexia*, from which the following selection is taken.

Dyslexia is a learning style with strengths and with weaknesses that require appropriate intervention. When this instruction is provided, students can learn. The following are important principles:
- People with dyslexia can learn and can become very successful in school and in life.
- It is never too late for proper instruction.
- Many strengths and gifts often exist as a part of this learning style. These are as important to consider as the weaknesses.

Dyslexia affects a person's ability to deal with language, including spoken language as well as written. A person with dyslexia can have difficulty understanding, remembering, organizing and using verbal symbols. Because of this, many basic skills can be affected, especially reading and writing, spelling, handwriting, and arithmetic. In addition, other issues can occur concurrently with dyslexia.

## Definitions of Dyslexia

There are hundreds and possibly thousands of definitions of dyslexia.

A serious and complete definition was adopted by the Orton Dyslexia society, renamed The International Dyslexia Association, an organization devoted to helping people with dyslexia, in 1994. This organization states:

> Dyslexia is a neurologically based, often familial disorder which interferes with the acquisition and processing of language. Varying in degrees of severity, it is manifested by difficulties in receptive and expressive language—including phonological processing—in reading, writing, spelling, handwriting, and sometimes in arithmetic. Dyslexia is not a result of lack of motivation, sensory impairment, inadequate instructional or environmental opportunities, or other limiting conditions, but may occur together with these conditions. Although dyslexia is lifelong, individuals with dyslexia frequently respond successfully to timely and appropriate intervention.

This definition is compact and contains a great deal of information and beliefs about dyslexia that are shared by this writer. To restate, dyslexia is not based on emotional or environmental factors but is a neurologically based condition that often occurs in families. Its level of severity varies widely among individuals. It affects language in general, and therefore the academic areas where language is involved, especially reading and written language. Occasionally mathematics is also affected. Even though poor teaching does not cause dyslexia, appropriate instruction can greatly help. Dyslexia can occur concurrently with other conditions, such as attention deficit disorder (ADD) or attention deficit hyperactivity disorder (ADHD), and people do not outgrow it. . . .

## Characteristics Associated with Dyslexia

People are often very confused by dyslexia, because it occurs in such different forms. There is no one "dyslexic" profile, no one standard set of characteristics. Instead, some students have speech articulation problems and halting verbal expression, while others speak fluently. Some experience eye-hand coordination immaturity, while others are able to assemble intricate puzzles and designs. Some seem to be in a world of their own, while others listen attentively and are very aware of social cues. Some cannot decode the simplest word, while others can read almost anything but have trouble comprehending what they read. Some reverse letters in reading and writing, whereas others do not.

There is also a great diversity regarding how strongly the dyslexic learning style occurs in individuals. Some people appear very similar to the typical learner in school. They may be a little delayed in learning to read and may experience some difficulty with spelling and grammar. Otherwise, they function very much like the rest of their peers. Other students can exhibit significant differences in many areas. They can be smaller physically and reach developmental milestones [later]; for example, the loss of baby teeth at a much later age. They can have difficulty with most academic areas and seem unable to cope with social situations.

This great diversity of types and levels of dyslexia makes it very confusing for teachers to plan educational programs. There is no one standard curriculum for all people with this learning style; instead, each individual has to be assessed and a program carefully developed that will maximize success. Diagnostic tests can be helpful in beginning this process, but the teacher often learns about which techniques work best while working with the student. . . .

## Common Myths

The most common myth, which is almost a stereotype because it is so widespread, is that all people with dyslexia reverse numbers and letters, and that this visual problem is the basis of the difficulty with academics. It is now known that people with dyslexia are as prone to reversals as anyone else, but not more so. In fact, children with typical learning styles commonly reverse letters and numbers until the age of seven. It is true that reversals can make written language confusing, but it is now commonly believed that the occurrence of reversals is neither a diagnostic sign nor a causal factor of dyslexia.

A second common myth is that people with dyslexia have impaired intelligence. In the past, IQ tests, which were largely based on language, were used to diagnose their needs. It is not surprising therefore, that they did not score well on these tests, because their problems are with language.

When an individual's needs are being assessed, it is critically important to find a diagnostician who is knowledgeable about how the dyslexic learning style affects test results. Then, true and helpful results can be obtained. It is now known that, most often, dyslexic people have average or above-average intelligence.

A third myth is that all people with dyslexia have ADD or ADHD. Although it is true that some do, this cannot be stated as a general rule.

A fourth myth, which is so very prevalent that it *is* a stereotype, is that gender is a factor, and that there are more males with dyslexia than females. Recent analyses have indicated, however, that this belief was based on studies that looked only at children who were already referred for services. New studies, which are examining large groups of children in school districts, are finding the same percentage of reading problems in girls as in boys. Many educators now believe that former studies are flawed because boys are more likely to be referred as a result of behavioral problems. It is also possible that some people still have higher academic expectations for boys than for girls.

As we turn to look at causes of dyslexia, therefore, many factors have been ruled out: It doesn't seem to be based on purely visual issues, on intelligence, on attention and behavior, or on gender. As educators, however, we commonly see students who seem so bright but who exhibit a wide range of symptoms—so what is causing their problems?

## What Current Research Is Showing

Educators and researchers have been examining the issue of phonological processing, also called *phonemic awareness*. This is the knowledge of the sounds connected with written language and the ability to manipulate them so that words and sentences can be created. It appears to be a common area of difficulty for people with dyslexia; they have trouble remembering the sounds of letters. Even if they know all the letters and sounds in a given word, they have difficulty putting them together in the correct order. Blending sounds is hard. Is it any wonder, then, that reading and other language-based tasks are difficult?

At this point in time, it is commonly believed that difficulty with phonemic awareness is a root cause of the reading, writing, and spelling difficulties. It is often noticed that children with dyslexia have had trouble focusing on basic language tasks, such as rhyming words, which seems to come naturally to children who have a more typical learning style. For students with dyslexia to be able to readily associate the sounds with letters, they seem to need carefully structured, extensive, multisensory instruction.

It's fine to say that lack of phonemic awareness is a common area of concern, but what causes this difficulty with isolating, identifying, and manipulating sounds? The development of such new technology as Magnetic Resonance Imaging (MRI) is giving researchers many new tools to search for the basic cause of dyslexia. It is now generally believed that physiological differences in brain organization and structure are at the root of the dilemma. Something is different in the way the brain processes languages, and researchers are working hard to find out what that is.

## The Revealing Brain

Fascinating work is now being led by Dr. Sally E. Shaywitz, a pediatrician and researcher at the Yale School of Medicine. Her research team uses functional MRI to see the brain in action—to observe the brains of people who are actually thinking and reading. While people are reading, rapid successive images of their brains are being recorded on a computer screen. The areas of the brain that are more active show up as brighter images because the blood is carrying more oxygen to those parts. Since it is now known where reading processes such as sounding out words and comprehending print occur, it is possible to map what is happening while people read.

According to a March 1, 1998, article in the *Hartford Courant* by Robert A. Frahm and Rick Green, in their most current work the Shaywitz team studied both typical readers and people identified as having dyslexia. Subjects were asked to perform such tasks as silently reading pairs of nonsense words and pressing a button for "yes" or "no" to say whether the words rhymed, while their brains were being imaged on a computer screen. The researchers discovered that the brains of people with dyslexia showed less activity in the area of phonemic awareness.

Researchers at Stanford University, however, have concluded that brain activity in the visual portion of the brain may be highly influential. A December 9, 1997, article in the *Hartford Courant* by Michelle Guido, Knight Ridder newspapers, reports that there was less brain activity in the visual portions of the brains of five students with dyslexia than in the brains of five students with more typical learning styles. David Heeger, assistant professor of psychology and neuroscience and the head of the Stanford research team, cautions that just thinking of dyslexia as an issue with the language center of the brain may not be the whole answer. There may be other factors that we have not yet discovered.

What, therefore, does research show us about the root cause of dyslexia? It is probably safe to say that most people now agree that there is a physiological basis for the condition. It looks probable that the language center of the brain is involved, but there may be other important physiological factors. Research will continue, and more truths will most likely emerge in time. It is important to discover the root cause or causes, because this has significant implications for educational methodology.

## Learning Styles

It is well understood at this time that people learn in different ways, and that we all tend to have relative strengths and weaknesses in obtaining and processing information. The primary ways that we learn are as follows:

- *Auditory.* Knowledge is gained and remembered through the sense of hearing.
- *Visual.* Knowledge is gained and remembered through the sense of sight.
- *Tactile-Kinesthetic.* Knowledge is gained and remembered through the sense of touch and body movement.
- *Analytic, or Left-Brained.* Knowledge is best gained and understood when individual facts are presented in orderly, sequential ways.
- *Global, or Right-Brained.* Knowledge is best gained when a general principle is presented, from which facts can be understood.

These ways of obtaining information are not exclusive. In other words, it would be a rare person, indeed, who used only one of the above modalities and approaches to learn. Every person, however, does have a pattern of typical ways through which she or he obtains and processes information, and this is called that person's learning style. Everyone learns fastest and most readily when this important individual style is considered in planning and presenting academics.

## Multiple Intelligences

In his book *Frames of Mind, the Theory of Multiple Intelligences* Howard Gardner presents a theory by which he identifies seven different types of intelligence. Each of these intelligences is associated with a well-defined learning style. They are:

- *Linguistic.* People with this type of intelligence are good with, or excel at, language and easily learn to read and write with traditional curriculum.
- *Logical-Mathematical.* Learners with this kind of intelligence enjoy figuring things out and discovering patterns in groups of data. They do well in science and math.
- *Spatial.* These learners like to look at things and are skilled at assessing spatial relationships. They can become fine artists.
- *Bodily-Kinesthetic.* People with this kind of intelligence often enjoy and excel with movement. They often learn best when they are presented with hands-on activities.
- *Musical.* These people understand and respond to rhythms and tunes. Music can be used to help them remember facts and ideas.
- *Interpersonal.* This form of intelligence fosters good social abilities and understanding.
- *Intrapersonal.* People with a good amount of this intelligence understand themselves and their own needs very well.

As with the various ways of obtaining and processing information, these intelligences are not mutually exclusive. People do, however, have their own patterns, and they tend to rely on some forms of intelligences more than others. Students with dyslexia tend to have relative personal weaknesses in their linguistic intelligence; this often causes them to fail with traditional curriculum. They can, however, have many strengths in their other types of intelligences, and these should be noted and used as educational programs are presented.

## The Strengths Associated with Dyslexia

Most teachers who have worked with students with this learning style quickly realize that they are privileged to be with students who have amazing talents. They can have uncanny abilities to fix mechanical things. In a small private school, one student was known for his incredible ability to locate objects. If anyone lost something, often the first words spoken were, "Go ask Pedro. He'll know where it is." And he usually did. A short list of specific characteristics often seen is as follows:

- Curiosity
- Willingness to ask questions

- Ability to look at things differently, otherwise known as creative thinking
- Good sense of humor
- Lots of energy
- Lots of drive and ambition
- Willingness to work hard
- Good mechanical abilities
- Good spatial abilities
- Good artistic abilities
- Good musical abilities
- Ability to focus for a very long time on a task that interests them
- Ability to recognize patterns in a group of seemingly unrelated data
- Ability to understand concepts

When we think about Gardner's concept of multiple intelligence, the so-called dyslexic learning style makes a lot more sense. These students appear to have relative weaknesses in some areas of linguistic intelligence, but researchers are coming to believe that this is primarily in the area of phonemic awareness. It appears that whatever causes this particular weakness also causes significant strengths in other areas of intelligence. For example, spatial intelligence is good, and that is why many students with this learning style can fix just about anything. Also, logical-mathematical intelligence can be excellent, and patterns can easily be seen.

It is interesting to think about the concepts of right- and left-brain thinking, which have been discussed so much in recent years. When we look at this model, we see how the dyslexic learning style relies so much more on the right-brain, global thinking, than the left-brain analytic thinking. A researcher in neuroanatomy, Albert Galaburda, who has been studying the brains of people with dyslexia, has found that, whereas in typical learners the left hemisphere of the brain is larger than the right, people with dyslexia have symmetrical hemispheres. The two sides of the brain also communicate differently than do asymmetrical hemispheres. This can account for the unusual weaknesses and strengths associated with this learning style.

## Gifted People

*In the Mind's Eye: Visual Thinkers, Gifted People with Dyslexia and Other Learning Difficulties, Computer Images and the Ironies of Creativity* by Thomas G. West is a fascinating book. According to West, the research shows that dyslexia is neurologically based and that differences in brain function create a wide variety of characteristics. This wide variety of characteristics is in itself a very important pattern. He states, "In the end, it may be that the most important and salient characteristic of the pattern is that each creative person is substantially different from the norm, the ordinary, but is also substantially different from other creative persons as well."

West also points out that the advantage of having a particular learning style is culture-based. A learning style that may be advantageous in one society may not be so in another. For example, in hunting-and-gathering cultures, people must have a good sense of direction and be alert and attuned to the variations in the natural world. Problems and challenges need to be creatively addressed. Reading and writing are not that important to survival.

I was recently in a university setting, where I had to find a person named Jeanette in a distant office. Because I got lost, she had to come and personally escort me to our destination. Jeanette commented, "I've noticed that writers tend to get lost when they're trying to find my office. They walk around, not noticing where they're going. It's odd." Linguistically gifted, but directionally challenged? Of course, not all writers are afflicted with this difficulty, but Jeanette did notice it as a common characteristic.

To summarize, West believes that people with the dyslexic learning style could have an advantage in hunting-and-gathering cultures, but in our current language-based culture, they suffer much trying to fit in. West further contends, however, that our society is changing—that with the advent of computers, we are being overrun with information, and people in business and other areas are struggling to deal with it. What is needed is an ability to see patterns in seemingly unrelated data, a creative way of approaching things, the energy and drive and ability to focus on a task long enough to solve a problem. According to West, in our future society, it may be the people with dyslexia who make significant contributions.

We must teach students with dyslexia well and have great respect for their abilities. They may be our leaders in future times.

## Famous People with Dyslexia

A great many individuals with dyslexia have already contributed significantly to our society: Albert Einstein, Winston Churchill, Charles Darwin, Galileo, and Leonardo da Vinci. Most of these people, of course, were not labeled as having dyslexia, because the term wasn't in use until the late 1800s. Also, it is only in recent years that we have a good operational definition, one that helps us recognize the learning style. As we look at those well-known individuals, however, recorded information about them causes us to postulate that they were indeed blessed with this special way of looking at the world.

We will look in more depth into the history of Albert Einstein, using information from *In the Mind's Eye*. I am grateful to Thomas West for presenting such a compelling and fascinating story of Albert Einstein's early life.

Albert Einstein's early development as a child was very slow, and he had particular difficulty with language. His sister has written that, in his early years, members of his family were afraid that he would never learn to talk. In a letter, Einstein states the following about his early schooling, "As a pupil I was neither particularly good nor bad. My principal weakness was a poor memory and especially a poor memory for words and text. Only in mathematics and physics was I, through self study, far beyond the school curriculum, and also with regard to philosophy." One of his teachers, an instructor of Greek, told him, "You will never amount to anything."

Einstein had a lot of musical talent, but he was very disorganized. He had difficulties with spelling and a lack of interest in learning facts. And in mathematics? Apparently, he consistently had trouble with mathematical calculations. When he was seven years old, he was known to get his knuckles rapped for not being able to give quick, rote answers to questions of multiplication facts. He knew how to solve problems, but he made lots of errors with the details.

Einstein's family moved from Germany to Italy when he was fifteen years old. The original plan was for him to stay in the German high school and finish. But, in his own words, "I was summoned by my homeroom teacher who expressed the wish that I leave the school. To my remark that I had done nothing amiss, he replied only, 'Your mere presence spoils the respect of the class for me.'

"I myself, to be sure, wanted to leave school and follow my parents to Italy. But the main reason for me was the dull, mechanized method of teaching. Because of my poor memory for words, this presented me with great difficulties that it seemed senseless for me to overcome. I preferred, therefore, to endure all sorts of punishments, rather than learn to gabble by rote."

Einstein was certainly not a star pupil in the traditional schools of his day. He did manage to get a university education, studying physics instead of mathematics. When asked about this, he answered that he had a stronger intuition in physics—that he was able to better see the important patterns in the midst of the many distracting facts.

When he graduated, however, he was not able to find a teaching job. Unfortunately, many of his professors felt that he was intellectually arrogant, and they did not recommend him for teaching positions. Einstein expresses his despair at this time: "After all, I am nothing but a burden to my family. . . . It would indeed be better if I were not alive at all. Only the thought that I have always done whatever lay within my modest powers, and that year in, year out I do not permit myself a single pleasure, a distraction save that which my studies offer me, sustains me and must sometimes protect me from despair."

How fortunate for our culture that Einstein had the perseverance to continue. How fortunate, also, that in 1902, a good friend of his helped him get a job in a patent office. Einstein used his free time to formulate papers and published them three years later. Once the world saw his work, he was recognized as the genius he was.

# WHAT CAUSES A LEARNING DISABILITY?

Joan Shapiro and Rebecca Rich

Learning disabilities are caused by biological factors, Joan Shapiro and Rebecca Rich assert in the following selection from their book *Facing Learning Disabilities in the Adult Years*. People with learning disabilities exhibit important differences in the structure and functioning of their central nervous systems, Shapiro and Rich write. The exact reason for this dysfunction of the central nervous system has not yet been determined, they explain, but possible causes include brain injury and heredity. While nonbiological factors such as home environment and school curriculum do not cause learning disabilities, the authors note that these variables can have a significant effect on how severe an individual's learning disability becomes. Rich is a professor of education and the director of literacy programs at the Westchester Graduate Campus of Long Island University in Purchase, New York. Formerly a professor of education specializing in learning disabilities, Shapiro is now in private practice in Manhattan.

A learning disability is often misunderstood. We have frequently been asked: What is the cause of a learning disability? Is it biological or due to the environment? Is it inherited?

We know that a learning disability is biological. During one's life, environmental factors such as schooling and personal supports can certainly make learning easier or more difficult, but the evidence shows that those who have a learning disability exhibit a subtle difference in the structure and function of their central nervous systems. This difference affects the cognitive processes that are essential to learning.

## The Role of the Central Nervous System

The complex and intricate communications network known as the central nervous system regulates and coordinates everything we do, including learning. The central nervous system includes the brain and the

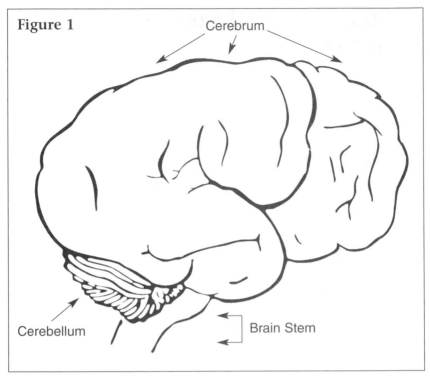

**Figure 1**

Cerebrum

Cerebellum

Brain Stem

spinal cord. The spinal cord relays messages, via nerve cells, between the brain and other parts of the body.

Learning is a function of the brain. The brain stem, the cerebellum, and the cerebrum are the key components of the brain (see Figure 1). The largest area of the brain is the cerebrum (located at the top of the brain), and it is here that higher thought processes such as memory, reasoning, and learning are centered. A large groove, or fissure, divides the cerebrum into two halves or hemispheres, the right and the left. While the two hemispheres are almost identical in structure, they differ in function. Structurally, both hemispheres have a strip of cells that control motor activity as well as four regions called lobes (frontal lobe, temporal lobe, occipital lobe, and parietal lobe), divided from one another by fissures. The strip of motor cells in one hemisphere controls the movements of the opposite side of the body. For example, the action of the right foot and hand originates in the left side of the brain, the action of the left foot and hand in the right side. A lobe in one hemisphere communicates with its counterpart in the other hemisphere through a bundle of nerve fibers in the center called the corpus callosum. (See Figure 2 for a diagram of the structure of the brain.)

The left hemisphere controls most language processing, as well as logic and organization, although information does flow between hemispheres. Each hemisphere has its own responsibilities, but for

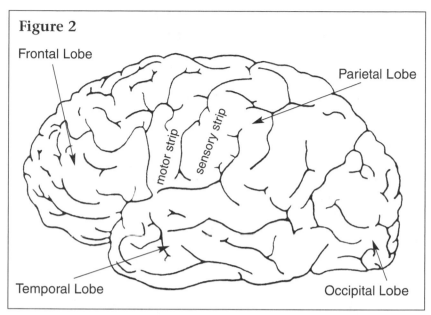

**Figure 2**

Frontal Lobe

Parietal Lobe

motor strip

sensory strip

Temporal Lobe

Occipital Lobe

most learning tasks the two hemispheres work together. Complex activities require the coordination of several regions within both hemispheres, each activated to a different degree. The right hemisphere is concerned primarily with nonverbal stimuli and directs such abilities as spatial perception, visual imagery, directional orientation, sequencing of time, and appreciation of art and music.

The brain is composed of 180 billion cells, 80 billion of which are directly involved in the processing of information. Each nerve cell has a cell body, numerous projections called dendrites that conduct impulses to the cell body, and an axon that directs impulses away from the cell body. Dendrites and axons of neighboring cells communicate with one another via chemical agents called neurotransmitters.

If a particular brain region is not functioning effectively, a person's ability to perform the tasks normally assumed by that area is diminished. The brain has billions of nerve cells, though, and sometimes cells from one region can, to varying degrees, take over the jobs of another. We refer to this phenomenon as the *plasticity* of the brain. The degree to which a person can recover from brain trauma is dependent, in part, on the person's age, the location and size of the damage, and the type and extent of rehabilitation or retraining the person receives. Despite the plasticity of the brain, complete recovery after brain trauma is the exception rather than the rule. For some behaviors there may be no recovery at all.

## The Brain and Learning: A Historical View

The field of learning disabilities has its historical roots in the work of physicians, psychologists, and educators who linked brain abnormalities to problems with language and language-based abilities such as reading and writing, as well as with a person's difficulty with perception, organization, and attention.

The term *learning disability* was first introduced to the field of special education in 1963 by Samuel Kirk, an educator, speaking at a conference for concerned parents and professionals. Dr. Kirk was looking to develop services for children of normal intelligence who were having significant difficulty learning and performing in school but who did not fit into existing disability categories like mental retardation, emotional disturbance, and sensory impairment. These children exhibited uneven patterns of development and had unique strengths and weaknesses in a range of academic and behavioral areas.

More than one hundred years before Kirk's talk, the literature described characteristics we now associate with the term learning disability and attributed these characteristics to brain dysfunction. As early as the 1800s, physicians, using autopsies of adults who had suffered from stroke, accident, or disease, discovered that damage to a part of the brain would result in the loss of the ability to speak. Somewhat later, connections were made between brain function and reading and writing, connections based on clinical impressions from work with children.

For example, James Hinshelwood, a physician, worked with children who had normal vision, motivation, and intelligence, but were unable to interpret written language. He termed their condition *congenital word blindness* and suggested that the problem was related to a specific difference in the structure of the brain. Samuel T. Orton, a neurologist, proposed that the lack of dominance of the left hemisphere, the predominant site of language, accounted for reading disabilities in children. Like Hinshelwood, Orton worked with children who had significant difficulty acquiring reading skills and whose reading and writing was marked by errors such as reversals of letters and words. He termed this condition *strephosymbolia*, meaning "twisted symbols." The constellation of characteristics both Hinshelwood and Orton identified is today associated with the learning disorder dyslexia.

## Understanding Brain Injuries

As one group of clinicians, like Hinshelwood and Orton, was associating brain dysfunction with reading and writing, another linked the brain dysfunction with certain behavioral symptoms. Kurt Goldstein, a physician treating World War I veterans, found that soldiers who had suffered head injuries showed perceptual impairments, distractibility and perseveration (being locked into producing the same action again and again), symptoms that persisted even after recuperation.

By the middle of the twentieth century, Alfred Strauss, a neuropsychiatrist, and Heinz Werner, a psychologist, were using information gained from research on the brain to better understand, assess, and teach children who exhibited characteristics such as excessive motor activity, poor organizational abilities, distractibility, perceptual difficulties, awkwardness with motor tasks, and perseveration—behaviors strikingly similar to those of Goldstein's soldiers. They speculated that the learning characteristics and behaviors these children exhibited were due to some form of brain injury sustained within the birth process. While some children did indeed have brain injury, for many, however, brain dysfunction was assumed on the basis of these clinical symptoms.

## Update on Research

Initially much of our information about the brain was based on post-mortem anatomical studies of brain sections. In the late 1970s and 80s, neuroscientists, most notably Norman Geschwind and Albert Galabruda, studied the brains of deceased individuals who were reported to have been dyslexic and found anomalies in language and language-related areas. More recently, advanced technologies have allowed scientists to study the working, living brain. Results of these studies have lent support to the autopsy findings. For example, research with magnetic resonance imaging (MRI), the neuroimaging device that transforms signals derived from magnetic fields into an anatomical image on a video screen, shows that the frontal region of the brain of children with dyslexia is different than it is in those without this disability. Similarly, work with brain electrical activity mapping (BEAM), which uses computers to map electrical brain waves, reveals that the electrical activity in the language-related areas of the brain of individuals who have dyslexia is different from those who do not have dyslexia. While the majority of research has focused on children, some recent work has been done with adults. In 1991, for example, Karen Gross-Glen and colleagues, using positron emission tomography (PET), which measures the metabolic activity of the brain, observed twenty-five adults with dyslexia as they performed reading tasks, and found significant differences in frontal and occipital areas of the brain.

Information about this work has been reported in the media, so it is not surprising that many people who suspect they may have a learning disability ask their doctors if this technology can be used to diagnose their problems. But these techniques are being used for research only, not yet to diagnose an individual learning disability.

Diagnosis of a learning disability relies on an assessment that uses a battery of achievement and cognitive tests to determine whether a significant discrepancy exists between ability and achievement. Given that technology is not yet available for clinical use, we have no hard-and-fast evidence of a central nervous system dysfunction.

## Causes of Brain Dysfunction

We have a number of possible explanations to help us understand why there are differences in the structure and function of the brain in individuals who have learning disabilities, but there is still much to learn. Prior to birth, during the birth process, or directly after birth, there may be some trauma to the brain, perhaps because of an inadequate supply of oxygen, nutrients, or blood flow. Or, perhaps, during the course of fetal development there is irregular development of the brain. We also know that the mother's use of alcohol or drugs during pregnancy may play a part. A genetic predisposition may also be a factor. And some individuals may have an imbalance in the neurochemistry of the brain. Research suggests a link between levels of neurotransmitters and problems with attention and impulsivity. . . .

Numerous studies conducted within the past thirty years, often in the form of family and twin studies, indicate that there is a 35 to 45 percent chance of inheriting a learning disability. Over the years, researchers have looked to identify a possible gene or genes that might be associated with a learning disability, but none has been isolated as yet. It is likely that more than a single gene accounts for the full spectrum of this condition, considering the heterogeneity of the population that has learning disabilities.

## Extrinsic Factors

As previously mentioned, extrinsic factors such as instruction, school curriculum, and home environment influence learning, but such variables do not cause a learning disability. The effect of the environment has been well documented in early intervention studies. We know, for example, that providing special education services to children younger than five years old who show developmental delays is crucial to support their capacity to learn. Beginning intervention when a child is older significantly reduces the ability to modify and encourage growth. In fact, we have a great deal of evidence that early intervention can accelerate cognitive and social growth and prevent subsequent behavioral problems. We spoke earlier of the plasticity of the brain. The younger the child, the more plastic the brain.

Intervention at a young age can also help the family, empowering parents to be an essential part of their children's learning and ultimately improving interactions between children and parents. With early intervention, some presenting symptoms can be overcome, others perhaps ameliorated, and secondary difficulties that can compound the disability, such as psychosocial problems, can be avoided. . . .

The school environment plays a critical role in learning. This includes the tasks we require individuals to perform, the learning setting we create, and the support we do or do not provide. These factors can greatly affect functioning at all ages and influence both short-term and ultimate success. Successful adults with learning disabilities have stressed to us the importance of these instructional factors. They have reported that small class size, availability of individualized tutoring, and teachers' willingness and ability to use a range of instructional techniques to accommodate diverse learning styles eased some of their learning difficulties and contributed to their achievements in later life. They knew they needed to work harder, and they benefited from teachers who used innovative approaches.

## Stress and Self-Esteem

Interactions at home, school, or work also affect self-perception and self-esteem, which in turn can influence learning. Research tells us that children and adolescents who have a learning disability tend more often to be rejected by both their teachers and peers than their classmates without the disability. Certainly such rejection would contribute to problems with self-esteem. In addition, a history of repeated academic failure may leave them with a sense of incompetence, low motivation, and unfavorable attitudes toward learning and school. Throughout their lives, individuals who have a learning disability may never know the satisfaction that comes from recognition, achievement, and affection. On the other hand, strong emotional support from family, friends, and teachers in the early years as well as in later life can help them enormously in dealing with academic and social/emotional challenges.

We know that at each critical stage of development, there is a shifting balance between *risk factors*, or stressful events that make a person vulnerable, and *protective factors*, which make him or her resilient. In order for a person to adapt well, there needs to be a balance between these stressful events, such as academic hurdles and peer rejection, and protective factors, such as emotional support from parents, teachers, and friends. And, of course, a person's individual pattern of strengths and weaknesses is a critical variable.

# A History of the Field of Learning Disabilities

Joan M. Harwell

In the following selection, Joan M. Harwell traces the history of
the field of learning disabilities, a discipline that she describes as
"relatively young." According to Harwell, learning disabilities
were not recognized as such until 1937; during subsequent
decades, scientists and educators greatly expanded the knowledge base concerning the various types of learning disabilities
and their causes. The treatment of learning disabilities has also
changed as new research has come to light, she notes. Harwell
has over thirty years of experience as a regular classroom teacher
and a special education teacher for students with learning disabilities. She currently serves as a field supervisor for student
teachers and interns at the University of Redlands and California
State University at San Bernardino. Her books include *How to
Diagnose and Correct Learning Difficulties in the Classroom* and
*Complete Learning Disabilities Handbook*, from which the following excerpt is taken.

The field of learning disabilities is relatively young. Historically, the
learning disabled person managed to cope—or didn't manage. I suspect that many persons with LD found jobs in unskilled labor or were
taken care of by their families. With the technological revolution of
the 1950s has come a demand for a better-educated work force. Geo-
graphic mobility and an increase in single-parent families are among
many social factors that have reduced the ability of families to care
for grown children. These dynamic social changes in society are
putting pressure on schools to do a better job educating all students.

Prior to 1937, there was essentially no recognition of the condition
we now call learning disabilities. In 1937, Samuel Orton, a neu-
ropathologist, used the term "strephosymbolia" to describe a problem
he had observed in children with reading difficulties, i.e., the reversals
of symbols such as *b/d* or words such as *saw/was*. He thought that this
might be caused by the failure of one hemisphere of the brain to

Joan M. Harwell, *Complete Learning Disabilities Handbook*. Paramus, NJ: The Center for
Applied Research in Education, 2001. Copyright © 2001 by The Center for Applied
Research in Education. Reproduced by permission of John Wiley & Sons, Inc.

establish dominance over the other, which resulted in mirror images of words and symbols. He noted that there seemed to be a continuum of reading disability ranging from mild cases to severe cases. The Orton Dyslexia Society was named for him.

The look-say method of learning to read in the early 1940s resulted in a high degree of failure to acquire reading skills. Samuel Orton [and educators] Anna Gillingham, Bessie Stillman, Romalda Spalding, and Grace Fernald responded to the need by developing alternative teaching methods for students who were not learning to read by visual approaches. Despite their pioneering efforts from 1940 to 1960, most students with learning disabilities were thought to be slow learners. It was rare that they received any special help. If they did, they were usually put into classes for the educably retarded.

## Breakthroughs in Treatment

Research findings in the 1960s were disturbing. Many children who had been classified as retarded were found to have normal intelligence when tested in a nonverbal format. William Cruickshank [an education professor at Syracuse University] suggested that their progress was being hindered by deficits in perception and deficits in attention.

A group of concerned parents of children who had difficulty reading met in Chicago in 1963 to discuss the needs of their children. At that time doctors referred to these children as being "minimally brain damaged" (MBD). These parents objected to the use of that label. [Educator] Samuel Kirk, who was at this meeting, suggested a new term, "learning disabled." The parents adopted the new term and established the parent organization for The Association of Children with Learning Disabilities (ACLD). They began to demand services for their children.

Shortly thereafter, the International Council for Exceptional Children created a division of the organization to address the needs of children with learning disabilities. By the late 1960s, education responded. Special education resource rooms were opened. Students were grouped for instruction according to their needs. Special educators tried to work on children's perceptual deficits and to help them reduce their distractibility. Research in animal and human behavior by [psychologist] B.F. Skinner and others led to a very different approach, "behavior modification," which became very popular in education during the 1960s.

Attempts to classify learning disabilities into LD subtypes began in the 1970s with the works of [pediatric neurologist] Elena Boder, [neuropsychologist] Byron Rourke, and [educational psychologist] Linda Siegel and have continued since. Earlier terms such as "dyslexia" gave way to reading disability, "dyscalculia" was replaced with the term arithmetic disability, and "dysgraphia" is now called writing disability. However, there has not yet been general acceptance of any subtyping scheme.

The most significant event of the 1970s was the passage of Public

Law 94-142 (The Education of All Handicapped Children Act) by Congress in 1975. It guaranteed that each handicapped child, age 3 to 21, would receive a "free and appropriate" education in the "least restrictive environment" possible. This law became known as the "mainstreaming" law. Children with LD were to be educated in regular classrooms unless the nature and severity of their disability was so great it could be demonstrated they could not make progress in regular classes. Each school was given the services of a Resource Specialist teacher (RSp).

Public Law 94-142 had one enormous shortcoming. It did not provide school districts with adequate monies to provide the services it mandated. At the time of its passage, it was presumed that approximately 2 percent of school children would require services. By 1987, almost 5 percent of school children qualified for services under the LD category.

Early in the 1980s, educational endeavors changed focus somewhat. Less effort was devoted to remediating perceptual deficits and the focus shifted to skills development.

About the same time, there was a resurgence in researcher interest in looking at learning disabilities. New technologies such as Magnetic Resonance Imaging (MRI) and Positron Emission Tomography (PET) were making it possible for the first time to map electrical activity and blood flow in the brains of living subjects as they performed various educational tasks.

In the late 1980s, the Regular Education Initiative (REI) encouraged special education and regular education to join resources. The Initiative said that students who had been served in pullout programs would be better served by their general education teachers in regular classrooms if their teachers had help from special education personnel. "Inclusion" was the buzzword. While the idea sounded great, teachers found it was difficult to put into practice. In classes where inclusion is a success, it attests to the flexibility and cooperation of the two teachers involved, because this is truly team-teaching. Resource Specialists were encouraged to spend more time with regular teachers consulting and collaborating about students' special needs.

Late in the 1980s, researchers suggested that the true causes of reading disability were deficits in phonological awareness, phonological encoding, and phonological retrieval abilities. This research strongly suggests that training in phonemic awareness and systematic phonics instruction are absolutely necessary for at-risk and reading disabled students.

## A New IDEA

In 1990, Public Law 94-142 was retitled and expanded. It is now called the Individuals with Disabilities Education Act (IDEA), Public Law 101-476. IDEA further refined the definition of a learning disability:

"Specific learning disability" means a disorder in one or more
of the basic psychological processes involved in understanding
or in using language, spoken or written, which may manifest
itself in an imperfect ability to listen, think, speak, read, write,
spell or to do mathematical calculations. This term includes
such conditions as perceptual handicaps, brain injury, minimal brain dysfunction, dyslexia and developmental aphasia.
The term does not include children who have learning problems which are primarily the result of visual, hearing, or
motor handicaps, of mental retardation, of emotional disturbance, or of environmental, cultural, or economic disadvantage. (U.S. Office of Education, Federal Register)

If you read this definition phrase by phrase, you see that it reflects
the historical development of the field. It also states who is included
and who will be excluded from special education services under the
label "learning disabled.". . .

## Children in Need

Many educators argue that the excluded child is being unfairly
deprived of essential services. For example, there are children whose
IQs fall between 75 and 85, who desperately need and would benefit
from more help, but do not get it because they do not fall into any
category of special education. Likewise, the child whose parents move
every few months is in desperate need of remedial help but many
schools have no programs available to address such needs.

Educators and parents look forward to the day when schools will
provide all children with whatever services are needed to help them
maximize their potential.

When you consider that:
- 60 million Americans read below eighth-grade level;
- 85 percent of juveniles coming before the courts are functionally
  illiterate;
- 50 percent of prison inmates are illiterate; and
- our continued prosperity as a nation depends on a better prepared work force, you suddenly realize that the cost to society of
  not providing effective education to everyone is enormous!

The pitiful status of education in the United States was the subject
of a government report entitled *A Nation at Risk*, published in 1983.
Following this report, parents blamed teachers and teachers blamed
parents. The length of the school day and school year were slightly
increased but achievement scores continued to be poor through the
1990s.

At the turn of the twenty-first century, a number of distinct trends
have emerged:
- A re-examination of our educational theories and practices. One

example of this is the movement toward combining the Whole Language reading approach with phonemic awareness training and phonetic skills development into a program called Balanced Literacy;

- A proposal for the development of a uniform, national achievement testing program;
- Stricter credentialing standards for teachers;
- An end to the practice of social promotion and tightening of the standards for promotion and graduation;
- Recognition by industry that it has a responsibility to provide parents with more family leave time, child care on work premises, and compensated time off for parents to help in their children's classrooms;
- The demand for reduction in class size has begun to be translated into action;
- Questions about the wisdom of the "severe discrepancy clause" which prevents earlier remediation with all students who need it; and
- A growing awareness that we need to provide more vocational training services in high schools for students who do not wish to pursue academic goals or cannot meet the standards for promotion. . . .

While the history of the field of learning disabilities has been of a short duration—about forty years—knowledge about the condition is steadily increasing. It is exciting to ponder what changes this new century will bring.

As educators and parents, we have a tremendous opportunity to influence children's lives. We have the power to make their days joyous or dreadful because we help determine the environment in which they live.

# CHAPTER 2

# ADDRESSING LEARNING DISABILITIES

Contemporary Issues
Companion

# DIAGNOSIS AND TREATMENT OF LEARNING DISABILITIES

National Institute of Mental Health

The National Institute of Mental Health (NIMH) is an agency of the U.S. government that conducts research on mental disorders and disabilities. In the following selection, NIMH describes the standard process of diagnosing and treating learning disabilities. Because parents are usually the first to notice signs of a delay in learning, the institute recommends that they should be watchful during their children's first few years of development. Once a problem has been identified, a formal diagnosis follows, involving a series of standardized and specialized tests. Most schools provide treatment for learning disabilities, NIMH reports, but parents may also choose to hire outside consultants such as tutors and learning specialists or to place their child in a special school for the learning disabled. In addition, the institute notes, government programs offer a wide variety of services to people with learning disabilities and their families.

Imagine having important needs and ideas to communicate, but being unable to express them. Perhaps feeling bombarded by sights and sounds, unable to focus your attention. Or trying to read or add but not being able to make sense of the letters or numbers.

You may not need to imagine. You may be the parent or teacher of a child experiencing academic problems, or have someone in your family diagnosed as learning disabled. Or possibly as a child you were told you had a reading problem called dyslexia or some other learning handicap.

Although different from person to person, these difficulties make up the common daily experiences of many learning disabled children, adolescents, and adults. A person with a learning disability may experience a cycle of academic failure and lowered self-esteem. Having these handicaps—or living with someone who has them—can bring overwhelming frustration.

But the prospects are hopeful. It is important to remember that a person with a learning disability *can learn*. The disability usually only affects certain limited areas of a child's development. In fact, rarely

National Institute of Mental Health, "Learning Disabilities," *NIH Publication #93-3611.* Washington, DC: U.S. Government Printing Office, 1993.

are learning disabilities severe enough to impair a person's potential to live a happy, normal life. . . .

## Case Studies

In this selection, you'll read the stories of Susan, Wallace, and Dennis, three people who have learning disabilities. Although each had a rough start, with help they learned to cope with their handicaps. You'll see their early frustrations and their steps toward getting help.

*The stories of Susan, Wallace, and Dennis are representative of people with learning disabilities, but the characters are not real. Of course, people with learning disabilities are not all alike, so these stories may not fit any particular individual.*

*Susan.* At age 14, Susan still tends to be quiet. Ever since she was a child, she was so withdrawn that people sometimes forgot she was there. She seemed to drift into a world of her own. When she did talk, she often called objects by the wrong names. She had few friends and mostly played with dolls or her little sister. In school, Susan hated reading and math because none of the letters, numbers or "+" and "-" signs made any sense. She felt awful about herself. She'd been told—and was convinced—that she was retarded.

*Wallace.* Wallace has lived 46 years, and still has trouble understanding what people say. Even as a boy, many words sounded alike. His father patiently said things over and over. But whenever his mother was drunk, she flew into a rage and spanked him for not listening. Wallace's speech also came out funny. He had such problems saying words that in school his teacher sometimes couldn't understand him. When classmates called him a "dummy," his fists just seemed to take over.

*Dennis.* Dennis is 23 years old and still seems to have too much energy. But he had always been an overactive boy, sometimes jumping on the sofa for hours until he collapsed with exhaustion. In grade school, he never sat still. He interrupted lessons. But he was a friendly, well-meaning kid, so adults didn't get too angry. His academic problems became evident in third grade, when his teacher realized that Dennis could only recognize a few words and wrote like a first grader. She recommended that Dennis repeat third grade, to give him time to "catch up." After another full year, his behavior was still out of control, and his reading and writing had not improved. . . .

*Susan.* Susan was promoted to the sixth grade but still couldn't do basic math. So, her mother brought her to a private clinic for testing. The clinician observed that Susan had trouble associating symbols with their meaning, and this was holding back her language, reading, and math development. Susan called objects by the wrong words and she could not associate sounds with letters or recognize math symbols. However, an IQ of 128 meant that Susan was quite bright. In addition to developing an Individualized Education Plan, the clinician recommended that Susan receive counseling for her low self-esteem and depression.

*Wallace.* In the early 1960s, at the request of his ninth grade teacher, Wallace was examined by a doctor to see why he didn't speak or listen well. The doctor tested his vocal cords, vision, and hearing. They were all fine. The teacher concluded that Wallace must have "brain damage," so not much could be done. Wallace kept failing in school and was suspended several times for fighting. He finally dropped out after tenth grade. He spent the next 25 years working as a janitor. Because LD frequently went undiagnosed at the time when Wallace was young, the needed help was not available to him.

*Dennis.* In fifth grade, Dennis' teacher sent him to the school psychologist for testing. Dennis was diagnosed as having developmental reading and developmental writing disorders. He was also identified as having an attention disorder with hyperactivity. He was placed in an all-day special education program, where he could work on his particular deficits and get individual attention. His family doctor prescribed the medication Ritalin to reduce his hyperactivity and distractibility. Along with working to improve his reading, the special education teacher helped him improve his listening skills. Since his handwriting was still poor, he learned to type homework and reports on a computer. At age 19, Dennis graduated from high school and was accepted by a college that gives special assistance to students with learning disabilities.

## Identifying a Problem

The first step in solving any problem is realizing there is one. Wallace, sadly, was a product of his time, when learning disabilities were more of a mystery and often went unrecognized. Today, professionals would know how to help Wallace. Dennis and Susan were able to get help because someone saw the problem and referred them for help.

When a baby is born, the parents eagerly wait for the baby's first step, first word, a myriad of other "firsts." During routine checkups, the pediatrician, too, watches for more subtle signs of development. The parents and doctor are watching for the child to achieve developmental milestones. . . .

Parents are usually the first to notice obvious delays in their child reaching early milestones. The pediatrician may observe more subtle signs of minor neurological damage, such as a lack of coordination. But the classroom teacher, in fact, may be the first to notice the child's persistent difficulties in reading, writing, or arithmetic. As school tasks become more complex, a child with a learning disability may have problems mentally juggling more information.

The learning problems of children who are quiet and polite in school may go unnoticed. Children with above average intelligence, who manage to maintain passing grades despite their disability, are even less likely to be identified. Children with hyperactivity, on the other hand, will be identified quickly by their impulsive behavior and excessive movement. Hyperactivity usually begins before age 4 but may not be recognized until the child enters school.

What should parents, doctors, and teachers do if critical developmental milestones haven't appeared by the usual age? Sometimes it's best to allow a little more time, simply for the brain to mature a bit. But if a milestone is already long delayed, if there's a history of learning disabilities in the family, or if there are several delayed skills, the child should be professionally evaluated as soon as possible. An educator or a doctor who treats children can suggest where to go for help.

## Formal Diagnosis

By law, learning disability is defined as a significant gap between a person's intelligence and the skills the person has achieved at each age. This means that a severely retarded 10-year-old who speaks like a 6-year-old probably doesn't have a language or speech disability. He has mastered language up to the limits of his intelligence. On the other hand, a fifth grader with an IQ of 100 who can't write a simple sentence probably does have LD.

Learning disorders may be *informally flagged* by observing significant delays in the child's skill development. A 2-year delay in the primary grades is usually considered significant. For older students, such a delay is not as debilitating, so learning disabilities aren't usually suspected unless there is more than a 2-year delay. *Actual diagnosis* of learning disabilities, however, is made using standardized tests that compare the child's level of ability to what is considered normal development for a person of that age and intelligence.

For example, as late as fifth grade, Susan couldn't add two numbers, even though she rarely missed school and was good in other subjects. Her mother took her to a clinician, who observed Susan's behavior and administered standardized math and intelligence tests. The test results showed that Susan's math skills were several years behind, given her mental capacity for learning. Once other possible causes like lack of motivation and vision problems were ruled out, Susan's math problem was formally diagnosed as a specific learning disability.

Test outcomes depend not only on the child's actual abilities, but on the reliability of the test and the child's ability to pay attention and understand the questions. Children like Dennis, with poor attention or hyperactivity, may score several points below their true level of ability. Testing a child in an isolated room can sometimes help the child concentrate and score higher.

## Specialized Tests

Each type of LD is diagnosed in slightly different ways. To diagnose speech and language disorders, a speech therapist tests the child's pronunciation, vocabulary, and grammar and compares them to the developmental abilities seen in most children that age. A psychologist tests the child's intelligence. A physician checks for any ear infections, and an audiologist may be consulted to rule out auditory problems. If the problem involves articulation, a doctor examines the child's vocal cords and throat.

In the case of academic skills disorders, academic development in reading, writing, and math is evaluated using standardized tests. In addition, vision and hearing are tested to be sure the student can see words clearly and can hear adequately. The specialist also checks if the child has missed much school. It's important to rule out these other possible factors. After all, treatment for a learning disability is very different from the remedy for poor vision or missing school.

Attention deficit hyperactivity disorder (ADHD) is diagnosed by checking for the long-term presence of specific behaviors, such as considerable fidgeting, losing things, interrupting, and talking excessively. Other signs include an inability to remain seated, stay on task, or take turns. A diagnosis of ADHD is made only if the child shows such behaviors substantially more than other children of the same age.

If the school fails to notice a learning delay, parents can request an outside evaluation. In Susan's case, her mother chose to bring Susan to a clinic for testing. She then brought documentation of the disability back to the school. After confirming the diagnosis, the public school was obligated to provide the kind of instructional program that Susan needed.

Parents should stay abreast of each step of the school's evaluation. Parents also need to know that they may appeal the school's decision if they disagree with the findings of the diagnostic team. And like Susan's mother, who brought Susan to a clinic, parents always have the option of getting a second opinion.

Some parents feel alone and confused when talking to learning specialists. Such parents may find it helpful to ask someone they like and trust to go with them to school meetings. The person may be the child's clinician or caseworker, or even a neighbor. It can help to have someone along who knows the child and can help understand the child's test scores or learning problems.

## Educational Options

Although obtaining a diagnosis is important, even more important is creating a plan for getting the right help. Because LD can affect the child and family in so many ways, help may be needed on a variety of fronts: educational, medical, emotional, and practical.

In most ways, children with learning disabilities are no different from children without these disabilities. At school, they eat together and share sports, games, and after-school activities. But since children with learning disabilities do have specific learning needs, most public schools provide special programs.

Schools typically provide special education programs either in a separate all-day classroom or as a special education class that the student attends for several hours each week. Some parents hire trained tutors to work with their child after school. If the problems are severe, some parents choose to place their child in a special school for the learning disabled.

If parents choose to get help outside the public schools, they should select a learning specialist carefully. The specialist should be able to explain things in terms that the parents can understand. Whenever possible, the specialist should have professional certification and experience with the learner's specific age group and type of disability. . . .

Planning a special education program begins with systematically identifying what the student can and cannot do. The specialist looks for patterns in the child's gaps. For example, if the child fails to hear the separate sounds in words, are there other sound discrimination problems? If there's a problem with handwriting, are there other motor delays? Are there any consistent problems with memory?

Special education teachers also identify the types of tasks the child can do and the senses that function well. By using the senses that are intact and bypassing the disabilities, many children can develop needed skills. These strengths offer alternative ways the child *can* learn.

## Individualized Programs

After assessing the child's strengths and weaknesses, the special education teacher designs an Individualized Educational Program (IEP). The IEP outlines the specific skills the child needs to develop as well as appropriate learning activities that build on the child's strengths. Many effective learning activities engage several skills and senses. For example, in learning to spell and recognize words, a student may be asked to see, say, write, and spell each new word. The student may also write the words in sand, which engages the sense of touch. Many experts believe that the more senses children use in learning a skill, the more likely they are to retain it.

An individualized, skill-based approach—like the approach used by speech and language therapists—often succeeds in helping where regular classroom instruction fails. Therapy for speech and language disorders focuses on providing a stimulating but structured environment for hearing and practicing language patterns. For example, the therapist may help a child who has an articulation disorder to produce specific speech sounds. During an engaging activity, the therapist may talk about the toys, then encourage the child to use the same sounds or words. In addition, the child may watch the therapist make the sound, feel the vibration in the therapist's throat, then practice making the sounds before a mirror.

Researchers are also investigating nonstandard teaching methods.

Some create artificial learning conditions that may help the brain receive information in nonstandard ways. For example, in some language disorders, the brain seems abnormally slow to process verbal information. Scientists are testing whether computers that talk can help teach children to process spoken sounds more quickly. The computer starts slowly, pronouncing one sound at a time. As the child gets better at recognizing the sounds and hearing them as words, the sounds are gradually speeded up to a normal rate of speech. . . .

## Increased Government Services

As of 1981, people with learning disabilities came under the protection of laws originally designed to protect the rights of people with mobility handicaps. More recent Federal laws specifically guarantee equal opportunity and raise the level of services to people with disabilities. Once a learning disability is identified, children are guaranteed a free public education specifically designed around their individual needs. Adolescents with disabilities can receive practical assistance and extra training to help make the transition to jobs and independent living. Adults have access to job training and technology that open new doors of opportunity.

The Individuals with Disabilities Education Act of 1990 assures a public education to school-aged children with diagnosed learning disabilities. Under this act, public schools are required to design and implement an Individualized Educational Program tailored to each child's specific needs. The 1991 Individuals with Disabilities Education Act extended services to developmentally delayed children down to age 5. This law makes it possible for young children to receive help even before they begin school.

Another law, the Americans with Disabilities Act of 1990, guarantees equal employment opportunity for people with learning disabilities and protects disabled workers against job discrimination. Employers may not consider the learning disability when selecting among job applicants. Employers must also make "reasonable accommodations" to help workers who have handicaps do their job. Such accommodations may include shifting job responsibilities, modifying equipment, or adjusting work schedules.

By law, publicly funded colleges and universities must also remove barriers that keep out disabled students. As a result, many colleges now recruit and work with students with learning disabilities to make it possible for them to attend. Depending on the student's areas of difficulty, this help may include providing recorded books and lectures, providing an isolated area to take tests, or allowing a student to tape record rather than write reports. Students with learning disabilities can arrange to take college entrance exams orally or in isolated rooms free from distraction. Many colleges are creating special programs to specifically accommodate these students. . . .

## Public Agency Support

Effective service agencies are also in place to assist people of all ages. Each state department of education can help parents identify the requirements and the process for getting special education services for their child. Other agencies serve disabled infants and preschool children. Still others offer mental health and counseling services. The National Information Center for Children and Youth can provide referrals to appropriate local resources and state agencies.

Counselors at each state department of vocational rehabilitation serve the employment needs of adolescents and adults with learning disabilities. They can refer adults to free or subsidized health care, counseling, and high school equivalence (GED) programs. They can assist in arranging for job training that sidesteps the disability. For example, a vocational counselor helped Wallace identify his aptitude for car repair. To work around Wallace's language problems, the counselor helped locate a job-training program that teaches through demonstrations and active practice rather than lectures.

State departments of vocational rehabilitation can also assist in finding special equipment that can make it possible for disabled individuals to receive training, retain a job, or live on their own. For example, because Dennis couldn't read the electronics manuals in his new job, a vocational rehabilitation counselor helped him locate and purchase a special computer that reads books aloud.

Finally, state-run protection and advocacy agencies and client assistance programs serve to protect these rights. As experts on the laws, they offer legal assistance, as well as information about local health, housing, and social services.

# HOW PARENTS CAN HELP CHILDREN WITH LEARNING DISABILITIES

Joan M. Harwell

Joan M. Harwell is a retired special education teacher who has worked intensively with learning-disabled students. She is currently a field supervisor for student teachers and interns at the University of Redlands and California State University at San Bernardino. In the following selection from her *Complete Learning Disabilities Handbook*, Harwell explains that children with learning disabilities need considerable supervision and advocacy from their parents. She describes the variety of ways that parents can play a crucial role in assisting the development of children who have difficulties with learning. According to Harwell, children with learning disabilities are aided immeasurably by parents who provide a nurturing and stable home environment, present stimulating activities, supervise homework, and encourage a diverse range of learning opportunities. In addition, she advises parents to work closely with teachers and the school system in order to ensure that their children's unique educational needs are met.

*During the preschool years, the family plays a major role in the child's cognitive and social development.*

The home is the child's first school and family members are its faculty. The first five years of a child's life are called the "formative years." For years, we have weighed the importance of nature versus nurture. A child is born with a genetic code that defines, in part, temperament and potential, but studies show that environment is critically important to a child's development.

Children who have parents who are warm, attentive, flexible, supportive, and accepting, and invest time in talking with the child, reading to the child, and teaching manners will find this attention is reflected in higher competencies throughout the child's life.

We know that when a child is born, the brain has trillions of cells. We also know that if these cells are not stimulated, they are pared away. We know that the optimal time for development of many cognitive functions such as language development occurs before age three. We also know that when this development does not take place during the optimal period, the child rarely catches up.

Parents create the environment in which the child is to be raised. Children benefit when parents find weekly time alone to discuss and plan aspects of their upbringing, and these planning sessions allow parents opportunities to develop a deeper relationship with each other. Children benefit, too, when parents are in agreement on how to raise them; contentious debates and divorces are particularly difficult for children who are learning disabled.

## The Home Environment

Even babies are sensitive to the atmosphere of the home. They sense tension and show anxiety. If there is yelling or other loud noise, they may become fearful. Their world does not seem to be a safe place.

Learning disabled children need more supervision so the decision as to whether both parents should work is a hard one. Where will the children receive the best care? If both parents are going to work, they face the challenge of finding quality child care. . . .

Parents have tremendous responsibilities for decisions about their children's lives. One decision they need to be in agreement with is how much television their children will watch and what kind of programming they will allow. The same is true of computer and Internet use.

There are interesting statistics on TV watching in children. Children who watch more than 10 hours of TV a week show lower school achievement. A study of children in one Canadian town, before and two years after the introduction of TV to their town, found that the children showed a decline in reading fluency and creative thinking, and increases in verbal and physical aggression. It is estimated that by the age of 18 the average child has witnessed 13,000 killings and over 101,000 violent episodes on TV. We are witnessing an increasingly violent society—is TV a main culprit?

The National Center for Education Statistics reports that when parents restrict television viewing, expect their children to make good grades in school, and talk with the child about future educational plans, the children are more likely to stay in school.

If a child has siblings, it is not unusual that they will feel jealous of the additional attention the learning disabled child receives. It is helpful if, when one is paying attention to this child, the other parent steps in and becomes involved with the other siblings.

Inevitably, there will be occasional squabbles. The child with learning disabilities should not be coddled or overprotected. With rare exceptions, that child needs the same parameters as the other siblings are given and similar consequences when guidelines are violated.

A playhouse and outdoor play equipment are great for 4- to 8-year-olds. Young children need objects to stimulate them, such as toys, books, and audio- and videotapes. . . .

If the amount of TV is restricted, which many experts advise, parents must consider what activities their children will do to occupy those extra hours. An activity-filled house is likely to become the neighborhood gathering place and will demand more parental supervision, but at least those parents will be able to supervise what their children are doing.

It is healthy for children to spend time without playmates at times and to learn to amuse themselves when alone. You can take them to the library where helpful librarians can guide them in the selection of worthwhile fiction and nonfiction books. Believe it or not, almost all children will pick up books and read if they have nothing else to do. Hobbies can be developed with some help from parents (the child's own or others). Drawing materials appeal to both boys and girls.

Look into after-school programs such as dance lessons, singing lessons, art lessons, and sports, that will develop physical skills. For the LD child, soccer is one of the best sports because good sportsmanship is encouraged and every child gets to play the same number of minutes. It is not wise to overschedule the child with activities every day of the week. The child will need extra help and time with school work. If you can afford private tutoring, look for a patient, nurturing tutor. Typically, the rate is between $25 and $35 per one-hour session. Listen to the child. If she indicates she is unhappy or uncomfortable, you may have the wrong tutor.

*Above all, know where your child is, what he or she is doing, and that he or she is being directly supervised by a responsible adult.* I remember one case where a 14-year-old had her mom drop her off several times at the church for youth group. Arriving early to pick the daughter up one evening, the mom went in, only to learn from the adult in charge that her daughter had never attended the youth group. Adolescents with learning disabilities are easily led into delinquent activities. The incidence of LD and juvenile delinquency among adolescents is high—ranging from 20 percent to 55 percent depending on the study cited. Watch for signs that may indicate the use of illicit drugs, including irritability, sleep disturbances, truancy, and covert behavior.

## Supervision of Homework

Parents of students with learning disabilities need to supervise homework through to completion. To do this efficiently requires a great working relationship with the child's teacher or teachers. *I encourage parents to ask the teacher(s) to call them immediately if their child does not turn in homework.*

Because these children often have trouble remembering assignments, *most will need an agenda or assignment notebook. Ask the teacher or a peer helper to write down all assignments and due dates.*

If your child comes home with the "I don't have any homework" story, it should be understood that he still has homework with you. *Listen to him read for 15 minutes.* One pleasant way to do this is to have the child read aloud while you prepare dinner. If something does not make sense, say, "Oops, please read that again, I didn't understand that." As the reading progresses, discuss what is going on in the story. When his "I don't have homework" is repeated two nights in a row, make a contact by phone or electronic mail with the teacher. Ask for a packet of materials that your child can complete at home when there is no homework.

What should you expect in terms of homework? Homework is generally given Monday through Thursday nights.

At grades K–2, homework should consist of some reading, spelling, and math. If the child applies herself to the tasks, it should take no more than 30 minutes to complete. Following are some time guidelines for the other grades:

- Homework at grades 3 and 4 probably will take 45 minutes to an hour.
- Homework at grades 5 and 6 will take about an hour.
- Homework at the junior high level usually takes about an hour and a half.
- Homework at the senior high level may take up to two hours.

If the child has an attentional problem, it may help to *break the homework session into smaller increments, with a short break or reward* following the completion of each task.

*If the child complains the homework is too hard, contact the teacher to ask whether that might be true.*

If the student has more homework than he can do in the time suggested above, talk with the teacher. Perhaps unfinished classwork is being sent home. In this case, *consider asking the teacher to prioritize the most important assignments or questions.*

Parents should provide their child with the tools needed to do homework, including crayons, colored pencils, glue stick, a ruler, and a dictionary.

Homework is ideally done in a quiet place, free of distractions and with good lighting and comfortable furniture. The TV should be turned off. If there are several children in the family, it may work to gather them at the kitchen table and have everyone do their homework there. As each finishes, review what was done before dismissing each to go elsewhere. If this proves too distracting for the child with LD, it would be best to set up a desk and necessary supplies for him or her to work in a quiet part of the home.

When the child sits down to do homework, *review the directions with him and be certain he knows what to do.* Ask him to explain to you what he is to do so you can be sure he understands.

*Always try to help the student with things she does not understand, but be wary if you are having to supervise her work every minute.* Many LD students have learned how to "con" parents into doing the work for them.

*Be lavish in praise:* "I like the way you are being so neat." or "That's a great sentence."

It is acceptable to reward children with money for completion of assignments, but limit this to no more than 50¢ a day for homework.

## Helping at School

Parents would be wise to spend some time each month in their children's classrooms in elementary school. This reinforces to the child that he is important and that education is important. It also can build rapport between a parent and teacher and allow the parent to see what's going on in the child's classroom.

If asked, many employers are willing to allow parents to take a couple of hours a month to do this.

When attending individual education program (IEP) conferences, parents should insist on a full understanding of what services are available to help their child.

## Advocating for Children

You are the most important advocate for your child, since you will be with them throughout their school career. The Individuals with Disabilities Education Act (IDEA) supports the right to be intensively involved in the educational planning for your child.

While most school personnel are well-intentioned people, many are overworked and, unfortunately, some are poorly trained or inexperienced. Be aware of your child's specific needs and be assertive in asking for things that might help your child.

Become knowledgeable about learning disabilities. Join an organization such as the Learning Disabilities Association. You may also want to join your school district's Special Education Parent–Teacher Association (SEPTA).

Attend your child's IEP meetings, ask questions, and offer solutions. Obtain copies of all paperwork and keep these records readily available.

If you and the teacher work hand-in-hand and have regular contact, your child probably will make steady progress in his skills. If you receive a poor progress notice, call for a special IEP review. Let your child know he can learn. Teach him to persevere. Do not make the child overly dependent by babying him and doing everything for him. Help your child take advantage of the vocational opportunities available through the school system. Insist that he have access to training in the use of the computer. You are the most important advocate in your child's life!

# ACCOMMODATIONS FOR COLLEGE STUDENTS WITH LEARNING DISABILITIES

National Joint Committee on Learning Disabilities

The National Joint Committee on Learning Disabilities (NJCLD) is an umbrella group consisting of representatives from a number of professional organizations committed to the education and welfare of individuals with learning disabilities. In the following selection, the NJCLD maintains that many people who have learning disabilities are capable of college-level work; in fact, the authors report, students with learning disabilities generally make competitive grades and usually take only one semester longer to graduate than do their nondisabled peers. Moreover, the authors stress, the success rate of students with learning disabilities can be increased if colleges and universities provide appropriate accommodations, such as textbooks on tape or alternative testing methods. The NJCLD urges institutions of higher learning to build campus communities in which students, professors, and administrators work together to enhance the educational opportunities for individuals with learning disabilities.

The National Joint Committee on Learning Disabilities (NJCLD) defines learning disabilities as ". . . a heterogeneous group of disorders manifested by significant difficulties in the acquisition and use of speaking, reading, writing, reasoning, or mathematical abilities. These disorders are intrinsic to the individual, presumed to be due to central nervous system dysfunction, and may occur across the life span. . . ."

Successful individuals with learning disabilities tend to be goal-oriented, determined, persistent, and creative. Persons with these characteristics are often an asset to the university community. Many students with learning disabilities are aware of their disabilities before matriculation. Some students, such as nontraditional and returning students, are not diagnosed with learning disabilities until after their admission to college. Once diagnosed, it is the student's responsibility

National Joint Committee on Learning Disabilities, "Learning Disabilities: Issues in Higher Education," *Collective Perspectives on Issues Affecting Learning Disabilities: Position Papers, Statements, and Reports*. Austin, TX: PRO-ED, 2001. Copyright © 2001 by the National Joint Committee on Learning Disabilities. Reproduced by permission.

to disclose his/her learning disability and the extent to which it affects academic access. A student's eligibility for services, and the particular type of service he/she needs, must be based on appropriate documentation. With appropriate accommodations it is more likely that students with learning disabilities will experience a successful college career. R. Witte, L. Philips, and M. Kakala in their study at a major university found that students with learning disabilities were competitive academically with their peers and graduated with grade point averages not significantly below the control group. This study also found that students with learning disabilities on average took only one semester longer to graduate.

## Institutional Mission

Presently, institutions are establishing learner outcomes for all programs. While students with learning disabilities should be expected to meet the institution's academic standards, they should be given the opportunity to fulfill learner outcomes in alternative ways. The process by which students with learning disabilities demonstrate mastery of academic standards may vary from that of the larger student body, but the outcomes can and should remain the same. Accommodating students with learning disabilities need not jeopardize the academic standards of the institution.

While the Americans with Disabilities Act and Section 504 of the Rehabilitation Act require institutions to make academic adjustments to provide equal access, they do not require postsecondary institutions to make changes to essential elements of the curricula and therefore do not compromise curricular standards. The courts and the Office of Civil Rights (OCR) have been clear that postsecondary institutions can and should establish policies that identify and maintain those essential components of the college curriculum. A team approach to reviewing the institution's mission and its policies for evaluating its essential programmatic elements results in a balanced and integrated plan for both academic integrity and educational access. Faculty and staff from the various programs can work to outline essential program components in relation to the institution's mission. Collaboration among administrators, faculty members, and disability service professionals should ensure that academic standards are delineated and maintained.

Although the team approach to policy design may involve a number of administrative offices, it is highly recommended that services for students with disabilities, including those for students with learning disabilities, be housed within the administrative structure that promotes a strong academic focus and shared faculty responsibility for providing accommodations. For some campuses that office reports directly to the president or provost; for others, disability issues may be under the purview of the academic or student affairs offices.

## Policy Issues

It is essential to have written policies that ensure that students with learning disabilities receive the same high-quality education as their peers. These policies should address the issues of admission, documentation of a learning disability, accommodations, and curriculum modifications. It is important that students be made aware of the existence of an appeal process which is set forth in writing. Students should have easy access to all written policies and procedures including the appeal process. Such documents should be available in a variety of formats, in all appropriate campus literature, and through available technology, such as a Web site, which all students can access.

*Admission Policy.* Colleges and universities vary in their admission requirements and policies; some have open admissions, while others have rigid entry requirements. Most students with learning disabilities meet the standard admission criteria and will not be readily identifiable during the admission process. However, some students with learning disabilities may appeal the standard entry requirements because of the effects of their disability on their academic performance or test scores. Within the appeal process for admission, available to all students, a mechanism is needed to consider the impact of a student's learning disability on his/her academic record. During the appeal process, it is important to recognize that inconsistencies in the student's academic record may reflect the presence of his/her learning disability. It is recommended that the admission appeal process for students with learning disabilities involve a team approach to decision making. It is imperative that the team consist of institutional representatives who are knowledgeable about learning disabilities.

*Documentation Policy.* As noted in the NJCLD definition, learning disabilities occur throughout the life span. Whether a college or university accepts a student's documentation as adequate or requires additional information before providing services, accommodation decisions should be addressed on an individual basis. The campus learning disability professional, in conjunction with the student, should evaluate the effects of the student's disability in relation to the curriculum and academic standards. During this process, faculty and other campus representatives may be consulted to review the academic environment and its relationship to the student.

## Accommodating and Adjusting

*Appropriate Accommodations.* A learning disability is not static; its effects may change in relation to a number of student, environmental, and curricular factors. Such factors as the student's abilities, the classroom setting, methods of instruction, or task demand may entail the need to provide differing academic adjustments. These accommodations, to be requested by the student, must be made on a case-by-case basis to ensure the integrity of the academic program and the educational experience. Requests for accommodations must be responded to in a timely fashion. The decision-making process for academic adjustments may involve the faculty member, the student, and the learning disabilities professional. Identifying and selecting appropriate accommodations require an analysis of the task, the student's disability, course objectives, and faculty input. Examples of accommodations may include but are not limited to the following: alternative test formats, extended time, alternative access to oral and written material, and course substitutions.

There are a number of new technologies and software options available that foster access to academic materials, such as text-to-speech, speech synthesizers, visual outliners, reading programs, textbooks on tape, print enlargers, visual tracking, phonetic spell checkers, and other emerging technologies. It is critical that technology on campus be reviewed and made accessible to students with disabilities.

*Curriculum Adjustments.* The federal laws and subsequent court decisions make it clear that colleges are not expected to make changes in the curriculum that compromise essential components of a program. In certain well-documented cases, a student may be unable to meet all of the requirements of a degree program. For example, a student seeking a bachelor's degree in nursing must complete all required courses in the program. However, if such a student had a history of poor performance in the acquisition of a second language that was directly linked to a learning disability, that student might then petition for substitution of a different requirement in place of the foreign language requirement.

Before course substitutions are considered, an evaluation of the course's purposes and outcomes should be conducted. Alternatives to course substitutions might include alternative testing, alternative evaluation of performance, and course audits. Because both the integrity of the academic program and the educational experience of the student are at stake, policy of this magnitude should be established and implemented through shared decision making. A team including the faculty member, disability service provider, student, and a learning disability specialist constitutes a balanced forum for decision making.

Acceptable course substitutions to be considered by college personnel include the following: culturally oriented courses, anthropology courses, or sign language in place of foreign language courses; logic, philosophy, or computer science courses as an alternative for a math requirement. The team making this decision should consider the individual's disability in relation to the student's chosen academic program. It should be noted that proportionately very few students with learning disabilities petition for course substitutions.

## Building a Responsive Campus

In recent years many questions have emerged during the development of services for students with learning disabilities: What documentation is necessary to determine eligibility for which services? What are the institution's responsibilities to modify a curriculum? What constitutes true access to education? S. Kroeger and J. Schuck give specific directives for creating a responsive environment. The authors call for organizing and structuring services, further defining access to higher education, clarifying of available sources and allocations of funding for services, and consistently evaluating services and the model for collaborating with faculty. Following are recommendations for building a responsive campus community to provide appropriate services to students with learning disabilities.

A. Review the Structure of the Institution
- Ensure that written college and university policy statements regarding services for students with learning disabilities are consistent with the mission of the institution
- Review all campus literature for statements of equal access and the procedures students with learning disabilities must follow to request services
- Consider housing the office for disability services in academic affairs or a similar administrative office for effective reporting and support

B. Establish Policies
- Ensure confidentiality of student information
- Develop written policies and procedures, including the appeal processes, regarding students with learning disabilities in the areas of admission, documentation, academic accommodations and curriculum adjustments
- Make policies and procedures available to the entire campus community via student handbooks, catalogs, and course schedules in alternative formats

C. Promote Awareness
- Establish mechanisms for dissemination of information about learning disabilities to students, administration, faculty, and service professionals
- Disseminate information to the campus community about available services
- Familiarize faculty, staff, administration, and students with laws governing accommodations for students with learning disabilities
- Clearly designate the individuals who make the decisions regarding accommodations so that intrafaculty or staff disputes are minimized

D. Collaborate
- Build campus expertise through collaboration and consultation
- Establish a team of service providers and faculty members for decision making in regard to admission, documentation, aca-

demic adjustments and program accommodations for students with learning disabilities

- Remain current regarding disability issues
- Provide cost effective, reasonable accommodations for students with learning disabilities

## A Campus-Wide Responsibility

The purpose of this paper is to provide recommendations related to institutional mission, policies, and accommodations for students with learning disabilities in higher education. Building an academic community responsive to diverse student populations, including students with learning disabilities, benefits the college community as well as society. Students with learning disabilities have individual strengths, weaknesses, and academic needs—as do all students. While it is important to consider individually the status of students with learning disabilities, it is critical that academic institutions plan for the admission and consequent education of these students. When colleges and universities examine their mission, develop policy, and work together as a campus community, education of individuals with learning disabilities can be greatly enhanced. Policies should address the issues of admissions, documentation of a learning disability, accommodations, and curriculum modifications.

Ensuring the education of students with learning disabilities is a campus-wide responsibility. Bringing the campus community together for shared decision making requires campus-wide awareness of students with learning disabilities, an understanding of the legal requirements for access, a review of essential program components, and a structuring of service delivery that is compatible with the school's mission. This institutional commitment and planning will allow students, faculty, and administration to work together toward their common goal: successful higher education for students with learning disabilities.

# CAREER PLANNING FOR ADULTS WITH LEARNING DISABILITIES

Raizi Abby Janus

Most adults who have learning disabilities are gainfully employed, explains psychologist and career counselor Raizi Abby Janus, yet many face substantial problems in the workplace due to their disabilities. Some individuals have specific duties that they find difficult to perform, Janus writes, while others are hired for positions for which they are ill suited, as in the case of a person with attention deficit disorder who takes a job that requires long periods of uninterrupted concentration. Janus suggests that career counselors should consider such issues when working with clients who have learning disabilities, directing them to appropriate careers that utilize their strengths rather than their limitations. Employers also need to learn more about learning disabilities in order to improve hiring practices and provide reasonable accommodations for their learning-disabled employees, she asserts. Janus is the director of assessment and counseling at the Personnel Sciences Center in New York City. She also teaches at the School of Continuing and Professional Studies at New York University.

If I was blind or in a wheelchair, people would know right away that I had a handicap, and at least they wouldn't always be blaming me. I get called undependable. I get called unmotivated. But I'm not. I do have trouble doing things quickly, but I've never missed a major deadline. I just can't do everything on the spot when my boss snaps his fingers. And it's true I have messed up some telephone messages. But it's not because I don't try; it's because some things I just can't do fast if I want to get them right. But people don't realize that. They think I purposely drag my feet or don't care. It's just the opposite: I work my tail off. I've tried to explain but no one wants to listen.

My boss says I'm making excuses. He just says that obviously I'm smart, so I could do everything I have to if I really wanted to. Last week he told me to read Steven Covey's book on *The Seven Habits of Highly Effective People*. And I did, a long time ago. Believe me, I am "honest" and "proactive." I'm "patient," and "virtuous." But I just cannot "make it happen." So my boss tells me to use my "resourcefulness" and "initiative."

But I do. I did. That's how I made it through college. I know I'm smart, but I also know I have a learning disability. I've got dyslexia and some memory problems—and now I've got a job problem because I'm about to get my walking papers.

The young man who told me all this was seated across from me at my desk. He had come for career counseling because his job was in jeopardy. Although he was dyslexic, he did not reverse letters when he wrote, and his learning disability had not prevented him from earning a college degree. Indeed, most people would say that he appeared completely normal. Consequently, beause he had no apparent abnormality, they often assumed that his problems were of his own making or "all in his mind." In fact, his problems *were* all in his mind, and that's why nobody could see them. He had an invisible handicap, and it is the invisibility of learning disabilities (LDs) that fosters the illusion that all is well.

## Moving Away from Normal

Learning disabilities are neurological in origin, hence they are invisible. They selectively interfere with the brain functions that control reading, math calculations, writing, motor coordination, and memory. Like LDs, attention deficit disorder (ADD) also originates in the brain. This disorder makes people susceptible to distractibility, impulsivity, disorganization, frustration, anxiety, and moodiness. Because LDs and ADD affect sensory processes, emotions, thoughts, and behaviors, they can pervade all aspects of a person's life.

In this discussion, I have used two politically incorrect terms: *handicap* and *normal*. Some people, especially those with a learning disability or attention deficit disorder, may be offended by my use of these words, but I have chosen them because they best describe the condition. LDs and ADD frequently are handicaps in the dictionary sense of the word: They "cause to be at a disadvantage, hinder, impede." People with these handicaps are not "normal" in that they do not "conform to the average of a large group," and being different in our society is often in itself a handicap. Indeed, disorders such as LD or ADD can be handicapping in all aspects of life and daily activities. They may inhibit social relations and undermine educational and vocational success. And they often present significant obstacles on the job, where procedures are designed for employees without disabilities. I shall continue to use these terms with the understanding that this is the intended context. In addition, for the sake of simplicity, I will use the male pronouns *he* and *him* for clients, and the female pronouns *she* and *her* for counselors. . . .

## Acknowledgment and Awareness

The "invisibly" handicapped client whose lament begins selection could have had a different story to tell. If his boss had been aware of the effects of a learning disability on specific job duties, he might have been more responsive. Instead of blaming his employee, he could have considered reasonable accommodations or task modifications. Then the young man, feeling less anxious and defensive, would have been more productive, and everyone would have been happier. But because he was not well informed, the boss began to think his employee was taking advantage of him. His irritability increased, and the atmosphere in the office became noticeably tense.

Thus LDs and ADD must be recognized and their effects understood if their consequences are to be mitigated. Adults with LDs and ADD number in the millions in the United States, and the majority are gainfully employed or seeking employment. Understanding the disorders and responding to the vocational needs of these clients will increase their chances of success. The best opportunities for creating "win-win" situations will come when everyone is informed and working together. LDers and ADDers must come to grips with their condition, and their counselors, job coaches, therapists, employers, and managers must be aware and informed. Each of these groups will be discussed in the pages that follow.

## LD and ADD Employees

In a competitive job market, LD and ADD employees are uniquely vulnerable because of the impact of their disorder. Companies in a cost-efficiency mode will be less inclined to dedicate time and resources on people with special needs. With guidance from a counselor, LDers and ADDers must determine the following:

1. What they can and cannot do, so that they can find jobs in which they will excel.
2. The most specific and cost-effective job accommodations, so that they can be as self-sufficient as possible and make the fewest demands on management for help.
3. The best way they can advocate for themselves, so that they can increase the possibility of productive outcomes.

Employees with an LD or ADD who are having trouble on the job often refer to self-help books intended for the normal population. But these books may be of limited usefulness for LDers and ADDers. For example, my client who had read and absorbed *The Seven Habits of Highly Effective People* had embodied the habits—all seven of them— yet on the job he was clearly not effective.

## Career and Guidance Counselors

Similarly, career and guidance counselors may provide inappropriate guidance if they assume that all their clients are normal. I have worked with many LD and ADD persons who have been through counseling in which well-intended advice was ill suited to their particular needs. Even though their interests and abilities may have been accounted for, their idiosyncratic disabilities were not. The results, as conveyed to me by these clients, have ranged from unsatisfying to thoroughly disorienting. Clients who have been led to believe that they have the interest and ability to perform a job well cannot grasp why they are unsuccessful. This kind of confusion erodes self-esteem and subverts the development of satisfying work habits.

On the other hand, counselors who are knowledgeable about LDs and ADD can improve the employment status of their clients in a variety of ways.

## The Counselor's Role

*Identify Strengths and Limitations.* Career and guidance counselors need to be able to distinguish between normal clients and LDers or ADDers to accurately identify each client's strengths and limitations with regard to emotional, intellectual, and social functions. The counselors can then equip their clients to decide what jobs are most suitable.

The counselor acts as an informed guide, pointing out to her client his strengths and limitations and how they interact in his daily life. For normal clients, going beyond this with a discussion of etiology could be irrelevant or even counterproductive. But if the client's limitations are caused by an LD or ADD and he is unaware of this, explaining the etiology of his problems is essential. For these clients to gain a clarified sense of self, they must have an awareness of the anatomical and physiological basis of many of their difficulties. Their learning disability or attention deficit disorder is intrinsic to who they are, affecting how they think, feel, and act. It may even affect their relationships with their peers. Because they are different, they need a different approach, and the counselor who can constructively demonstrate her client's strengths while explaining his limitations will increase his chances for success.

Of course, some clients enter an assessment fully aware of their disorder and able to accept its consequences. They will be most comfortable with a well-informed counselor who understands the implications of LD and ADD.

*Impart a Sense of Control.* Knowledge of LDs and ADD enables the counselor to help her client increase his sense of control and reduce his insecurities. She understands his psychological state and is able to respond accordingly.

Many LD and ADD clients believe they are as smart as others who are more successful. But try as they may, they "can't get their act together." They ask, "If I'm so smart, how come I'm so stupid?"

This state of confusion deprives them of feeling they can control their behavior or predict its outcome. They are uncertain about when they will perform well and when they will fail. Furthermore, they do not even know *why* they fail. This general sense of insecurity results in an even lower self-esteem.

When a counselor tells a client explicitly that he has an LD or ADD, there is a risk that he could feel ashamed of the label. But when he is told in a proper setting and with genuine concern for his welfare, most often a sense of relief ensues. He can see his invisible handicaps for what they are: part of a syndrome with well-defined symptoms that can be dealt with.

Knowing the cause of his problems, and when they are liable to surface, increases his ability to predict and control outcomes. This bolsters a feeling of security and helps prevent continued erosion of self-esteem. Attributing problems to a specific disorder defines parameters of its effects and puts the vague and inexplicable into a concrete realm. It permits realistic facts to ease doubts about what can and cannot be achieved.

## Working Toward Success

*Reinforce a Positive Concept of Self.* With an understanding of the disorders, the counselor can provide the basis for a positive refraining of the LD/ADD client's self-concept. She can encourage him to understand that failures are not caused by some global flaw, his failure as a human being. He is not "lazy," "careless," or "stupid." Rather, his academic and vocational problems have their basis in physiological disorders. Ineffective performance can be viewed as an operational glitch resulting from the LD or ADD in an otherwise sound system.

A restructuring of self-perception on the most positive foundations possible is basic to progress for many LD/ADD clients. Their sense of self can be reframed to emphasize actual potential and possibilities for growth. It becomes easier to highlight strengths when limitations are placed within clear lines of demarcation. Strengths are foregrounded, and weaknesses are seen as innate constraints imposed by the disorder.

A counselor should help the client understand that people may be held responsible for not trying to maximize their strengths, but they are not to blame for inborn deficits. This allays guilt and anxieties about past failure and provides a positive focus for future efforts.

*Set Appropriate Levels of Expectation.* An informed counselor can set reasonable levels of expectation for her LD/ADD client. In emphasizing strengths, she encourages him to hold high standards for achievement, but this must be done with a realistic and balanced approach that acknowledges his limitations. Otherwise, the client could set himself up for failure. In LD or ADD career assessment, the counselor must be concerned with more than the "minimal aptitude needed for successful performance," [writes R. Lowman in *The Clinical Practice of Career Assessment*]. Minimal aptitude is often not enough to withstand the interference in function caused by a learning disability or attention deficit disorder. Indeed, maximum aptitude may not be enough.

A factor that relates to the ADD client in particular is drug therapy. Although the counselor cannot allow the client to expect more than he is physiologically able to deliver, ADD physiology can often be given a boost with medication.

To illustrate this point, consider someone who is intelligent, analytical, detail oriented, meticulous, patient, and fascinated by medical research. He could become a medical lab researcher with expertise in microscopy—that is, if he had good vision or if his vision were correctable with glasses. But what if his vision remained unclear even when corrected? A counselor would certainly steer him away from any work that required visual acuity.

Visual deficits are an obvious constraint on microscopy. Less obvious are the constraints imposed by attentional deficits, yet some jobs cannot be performed adequately when these problems exist. Just as the integrity of the sensorium must be taken into account for certain jobs, so, too, the integrated functioning of the attentional systems. If these systems are dysfunctional, pharmacological remedies may be able to sharpen attentional acuity.

Drug treatment for ADD is not likely to result in as instantaneous and complete a success as the use of glasses for correcting poor vision. It may not help at all. The counselor needs to assess the impact of this disorder on the client's function—without as well as with medication—to avoid suggesting jobs that would demand concentration or perseverance beyond his capacity, and to avoid precluding jobs that he could manage with appropriate medication. . . .

## Job Coaches and Therapists

A job coach who is not fully aware of the involuntary nature of many of the problems associated with these disorders will attain limited results with clients who are affected. The coach may offer the usual solution for a common problem and then find that it is solved only temporarily or not at all. For example, a coach can teach the client principles for organizing a particular project, which the ADD client then uses successfully. But the client has difficulty generalizing the principles, and in a new situation he does not know where to start. He cannot put it all together on his own. In fact, the ADDer may have to learn the principles all over again for each new task. He needs to be "walked through" projects more often and for a longer period than other clients.

Therapists who treat a variety of ailments should have a complete picture of the problems that LDers and ADDers have in school and the workplace. Often, these clients' inability to achieve creates a pervasive sense of incompetence, which can be as devastating as poor parenting for their ego development. The failure to recognize LD or ADD can also cause unnecessary hardship for family members. Uninformed therapists may admonish the parents of an LD student for being "too involved" or "not involved enough"—or some variation of "too" or "not enough." The remorse felt by these parents is often equaled by their confusion as to how and when they went wrong.

## Employers and Managers

Companies that lift their sights above the "bottom line" to seek worker satisfaction need to know about the handicaps of LD and ADD. Employers, supervisors, and human resources personnel may not realize that a particular employee has an LD or ADD—or what its effects may be. However, it is essential that they know about these handicaps in order to respond to each person's needs. This awareness can improve hiring practices, personnel training and development, conflict resolution, and career management procedures. Finally, it sets the stage for a company to maintain forward-looking and humane personnel practices alongside a high standard of productivity.

*Nondiscriminatory Hiring Practices Versus Discriminating Selection Procedures.* Hire the Handicapped was a well-known slogan until the word *handicap* was jettisoned in the name of political correctness. Nonetheless, countless companies continue to respond to this slogan.

When hiring the handicapped, companies must use selection procedures that are both discriminating and nondiscriminatory. To select the candidate with the best job qualifications while avoiding all discrimination on the basis of specific handicaps is difficult. For the sake of fairness, businesses must invite every potentially qualified person to apply for the jobs available, and they must provide accommodations in the selection process so that handicapped applicants can have an equal opportunity. Indeed, these fair practices have been mandated by law. The selection process must identify the applicants who can most effectively discharge the job functions.

Equal opportunity does not, however, translate into equal suitability for every job. Some duties might seem easy, but not all employees can perform them equally well. Even for a simple clerical assignment, a discriminating placement of employees is necessary. For example, an uncomplicated and concrete service such as copying papers according to the customer's particular request requires a courteous demeanor, listening skills, organizational ability, and attention to detail. A person without these skills cannot perform this task well. Having been a customer on the receiving end of a poorly delivered service, I can attest to this.

## A Personal Anecdote

One day, before going to work, I went to an office supply store to get several articles copied. Each article was about five or six pages long,

and I needed twelve copies of each. They were to be copied in a speci-
fied order that followed the outline of the seminar I was presenting,
and then they were to be collated and stapled. I was pressed for time,
anxious to hand over the papers, give quick instructions, and get to
my first appointment on schedule. The young woman behind the
counter looked up from the copy machine and acknowledged my presence but did not move in my direction or say anything. Somewhat
annoyed at her nonchalance, I informed her that I was in a hurry and
asked her to please take my articles. She responded "Okay," but she did
not budge from the machine for several minutes. I took stock of her
when she finally came over. She was tall, thin, and somewhat stooped.
Her nails were bitten down, with their red nail-polish peeling.

I explained to her what I needed, and she gazed at me as I spoke.
But instead of responding, she seemed to follow some internal direc-
tive and returned to the copy machine without uttering a word. I was
taken aback, but as I expected her to return any instant, I said nothing. It must have taken fully two minutes before she again ap-
proached and asked for a second time what I needed.

My mood was deteriorating with each tick of the clock, but her
downtrodden appearance compelled patience. I repeated my instructions. This time she responded with a detailed description of the copy
machine's functions, which I assumed was confirmation that she
could fulfill my request. But this was only an assumption. I could not
follow her explanation, and two more repetitions did not help. Now I
was feeling irritated, pressured, guilty, and confused. Even more
uncomfortable was the creeping sense of foreboding.

Taking no chances, I told her three times that I would need to have
the articles copied in the exact order in which she received them; I
pointed out that the articles were numbered and that there was a
paper clip holding each article together; I told her twice that I wanted
the clipped papers to be stapled as a unit; I wrote down on a separate
pad exactly what I had told her; and I emphasized that she could refer
to these instructions as often as she needed.

She replied that it would be two hours before she could get to the
job, so I would have to come back later to pick it up. It was late afternoon when I returned. I needed to pick up my papers and leave quickly.

The first ominous sign was the perplexed look on the face of the
young man who went to fetch my papers. He stood in front of the
shelf where my job should have been, ruffling the papers inside. Since
there was no trace of my originals or the copies in the "J" cubbyhole,
he scanned the entire alphabet of cubbies. I stood behind the counter
with a queasy stomach as another young staffer joined the search.
After ten minutes of rummaging, they found both the articles and the
copies. My wallet out, ready to pay and run, I was very relieved. But
the situation had become ripe for a full blossoming of Murphy's law:
The papers were not collated, nor were the pages of all the articles in

order. The beginnings and endings of several had been randomly interchanged. Some articles had grown, and others had shrunk.

All the clerks were busy with customers, and my perpetrator had left for the day. I would have to wait for someone to re-sort the papers and complete the job. Awash in feelings of frustration and anger, I started re-sorting, collating, and stapling the papers myself, a task that took more than an hour. I fumed, counted, reorganized, stapled, got multiple paper cuts, and vowed never to go there again.

Later, when I handed out the articles, the incident provided the perfect introduction to the seminar, entitled "Learning Disabilities in the Workplace." I was able to convey the details of my mishap with the vivid emotion of one who had recently lived through it. The participants listened intently; almost everyone in the room could recall a similar experience.

## Guaranteed Failure

Thinking about my reactions as the incident unfolded, I knew this was a trivial bleep on the screen of my life's events. Nonetheless, it was unnecessary and a waste of time. And the service promised by the store had not been delivered.

My experience with this young woman could probably be multiplied many times for other customers. Some might surmise sympathetically that she had a problem or handicap, that her social awkwardness and clerical errors were not intentional. Some might complain to the manager, asking why the store chose to hire her and promising not to come back for a second dose. Still others might express their displeasure directly to the employee.

Perhaps this young woman had an auditory-processing disorder that affects her assimilating, sequencing, and organizing language as she speaks and hears it. Perhaps she also had ADD, which could have made her skip a few beats, get things out of order, and not notice. How much better it would have been if an employee without this particular combination of disorders had taken my request—better for me, better for the store, better for her. She was hired for a job that guaranteed failure because of her intrinsic cognitive limitations. The company was guilty of benign neglect, as it neither placed her in the right position nor provided her with a supervisor to guide and monitor her work. The young woman, the customer, and ultimately the store's profits bear the brunt of the store's deficient hiring, managing, and training procedures.

A prehiring survey of the company would have identified the positions available and the specific tasks of each. An assessment of the young woman would have uncovered her relevant strengths and limitations. With this information, the prospective employee could have been matched to a suitable job. If the young woman's skills had been appropriately used, the company's needs would have been better met.

Greeting customers appropriately, running off copies, and organizing and filing them requires certain skills that not everybody has, even highly intelligent people.

All too often, if a learning disability is not taken into account, it becomes an impediment. Frequently, it is the simplest tasks that LD or ADD individuals find difficult. But even the simplest tasks may be important to keeping an organization running smoothly—from maintaining supplies of copy paper and stamps, to taking down telephone numbers correctly.

This young woman needed a job with minimal customer contact and sequential, rather than simultaneous, task requirements. She needed a job that would use her strengths and not her limitations. For example, she could have worked in the stockroom, filing and locating orders, one at a time and without pressure. This would have enabled her to perform better, and it would not have jeopardized customer service in the store.

## Raising Awareness

*Invisible handicaps* need to be perceived and their consequences for the workplace understood. Indeed, a general awareness-raising with regard to LD and ADD, by talking about these disorders, educating practitioners, the business community, and the public about them, will go a long way toward normalizing them. The more commonplace they become in the public mind, the easier it will be to deal productively with them, and the less likely that they will be handicapping conditions.

# LEARNING DISABILITIES IN THE WORKPLACE

Gary F. Beasley

Learning disabilities can have serious ramifications for companies, according to Gary F. Beasley, the training manager for Georgia-Pacific's Crossett Paper Operations in Arkansas. For example, he explains that at his corporation, workers with dyscalculia, a math disability, made calculation errors that cost the company a million dollars. However, Beasley reports, Georgia-Pacific has had considerable success in addressing such problems after instituting a workplace education program to correctly diagnose and help employees who have learning disabilities. He points out that most companies do not have similar programs, nor do they realize that learning disabilities can negatively impact their profit margins. Beasley urges businesses to increase their awareness of learning disabilities and create programs to help learning-disabled employees improve their performance in the workplace.

I am the Training Manager at one of Georgia-Pacific's sites in southeastern Arkansas, which represents about 1,800 employees. The entire corporation has approximately 60,000 employees.

There are five areas that we're working on concerning education, vocational education and learning disabilities (LD), and experiences in the workplace. First, I would like to put our efforts in context.

*Success in Training.* We have an extensive technical training program throughout our organization that focuses on a "success in training" approach—training to successfully compete and progress through the jobs in the organization. We have a certification and qualification process whereby we do extensive training of all employees and prospective employees. We spend approximately $4 million–$5 million per year just on in-plant training for our work force.

*Upgrading Standards.* In our overall training, we are continually upgrading the skills of our employees and examining how to upgrade standards for prospective employees. The global economy demands that we have the best-trained employees possible. It is problematic to

Gary F. Beasley, "Center for Excellence: Learning Disabilities in the Workplace," *Learning Disabilities: Lifelong Issues*, edited by Shirley Cramer and William Ellis. Baltimore, MD: Paul H. Brookes, 1996. Copyright © 1996 by Paul H. Brookes Publishing Company, Inc. Reproduced by permission.

determine what skills, capabilities, and prospective abilities employees need. At present, we are using a 12th-grade reading, writing, and math test, and an individual would not be employed by Georgia-Pacific without scoring a 12.9-grade equivalent on that test. In addition, every person has to spend 40 hours in training before coming into the plant, and this is done through our vocational division. All maintenance employees at our site have to complete 2 years of technical training in mechanical maintenance or electrical instrumentation programs. This is a joint program that Georgia-Pacific has developed at our site in cooperation with vocational schools and other businesses in the area.

In 1996–1997, the entry-level qualification for any job in our mill is completion of a 2-year postsecondary program, either pulp and paper or industrial processes, each of which includes chemistry, physics, and mathematics. When high standards are developed for employees and prospective employees, it causes some problems. What do you do with people who do not reach those levels? In addition to new employees, we also require the same standard in reading, writing, and math skills at the 12th-grade level for transferring employees. This requirement cannot be met by someone with only a high school diploma—we actually test reading, writing, and math levels.

## Identifying and Helping Workers with Learning Disabilities

When we began the program with our employees, we found significant problems. We found that 45% of them could not reach this level in reading, writing, and math. In terms of prospective employees, approximately 60% could not reach the 12th-grade standards. This is about our community, but there are similar statistics in workplaces across the country. We feel we have higher potential in the workplace than many other communities do.

We began our program in 1990, and by the end of 1993 approximately 78% of our employees reached a 12.9-grade equivalent in reading, writing, and math. We worked with adult education and literacy programs and also a workplace education program to provide the training. We would not require these tests until we had the systems in place to help our employees and prospective employees reach the desired educational level. We formed our workplace education program.

When approximately 20%–22% could not reach the 12th-grade level, something started happening. We questioned why they could not reach this level. We saw that people were studying longer and becoming frustrated. They could not quite get there. We set about trying to determine how we could help these employees. So in 1993, we set up a project to help those employees with LD. At the time, we checked on what had been done in the workplace for those with LD and we did not find any other companies with LD programs that addressed the work force actually on an industrial site. We then began using learning inventories and getting help from professionals in observation and diagnostics. Eventually, we started a statewide LD program to help other workplace efforts.

In 1994, we were at the end of the first year of this LD program, and we were making assessments about the tools and techniques that we had found helpful for employees in the workplace. We look forward to sharing our conclusions with other employers. From our experience, there are many things that cause problems for workers with LD. For example, we discovered that we have a $1 million inventory of parts that have been misordered. If you misplace $1 million worth of parts, you investigate. We found out that dyscalculia was the culprit. The problem was that these employees inverted, flipped, or misarranged the numbers, entered the information into the computer, and then the parts were delivered. It cost us $1 million in incorrectly ordered parts.

At Georgia-Pacific, we have a participatory management process in which decisions are made by employees at all levels. As you can imagine, more employees are responsible for decisions and 10%–15% of them have LD. You can imagine the problems that this management style could cause us in terms of bottom-line costs and profits. We are trying to set up programs so that we can start addressing these issues.

## Key Considerations

There are some key points that need to be considered as far as workplace programs are concerned, and I want to identify some issues that should be addressed in the future. One of the key points that we need to examine is that most businesses and industries have no idea of the literacy levels of their employees, let alone the ramifications of LD. Most businesses and industries do not know how to go about measuring literacy levels. Industry and labor leaders need help with measuring literacy, and they need to understand LD and what opportunities exist for employees and prospective employees. Most businesses in Arkansas—and I cover the whole state as a vocational education board member—do not even recognize the terms when I talk about them. Cost control and profitability will suffer until we address the 10%–15% of our work force with LD.

Another consideration is that educators and workplace education programs need help in identifying workers with LD. We are trying to develop better identification processes. We need to help workers develop some self-awareness so that they can get help. This will also improve job performances.

Electronic media are great tools, but there are some problems with them. If you cannot read, or take the correct information off the paper, or the information changes in your mind before you speak it or enter it in that computer, electronic media are of no help.

# Room for Improvement

In terms of the future, we need to research, develop, and publish appropriate accommodations. When we used the Test of Adult Basic Education (TABE) and asked the publisher for appropriate accommodations, we were told they did not have any. We need to have lists of appropriate accommodations that will not compromise test integrity.

We also need to consider strategies for addressing LD in the private sector, and these strategies need to be formulated in a way that will minimize employers' exposure to lawsuits. We need public awareness so that the implications of LD are better understood.

We need linkages between professional diagnostic resources and educational practitioners. We can identify problems, but we need ways to help people. Whether through observation or assessment, we need to help students understand that they have LD and should not be afraid of it, so that they can go to their jobs and have employers who will help them perform in the workplace.

CHAPTER 3

# TEACHING STUDENTS WITH LEARNING DISABILITIES

Contemporary Issues
Companion

# THE IMPORTANCE OF TEACHER PREPARATION

National Joint Committee on Learning Disabilities

Founded in 1975, the National Joint Committee on Learning Disabilities (NJCLD) is a national coalition of organizations dedicated to the education and welfare of individuals with learning disabilities. In the following report, the NJCLD emphasizes the importance of preparing prospective teachers to address the needs of students with learning disabilities. According to the committee, general education teachers should have a thorough grounding in how to identify and instruct students with learning disabilities because the majority of these children are placed in general education classrooms. Special education professionals should receive additional in-depth training covering the diverse range of learning disabilities and specialized methods of evaluation and instruction, the NJCLD recommends.

The National Joint Committee on Learning Disabilities (NJCLD) believes it is essential that educators be prepared to meet the needs of all students, including students with learning disabilities who have unique needs. The NJCLD believes that comprehensive, interdisciplinary programs are necessary to ensure adequate preparation of professionals in education. Only then will there be the healthy exchange of ideas that will lead to a more complete view of how individuals learn. An interdisciplinary approach promotes the development and use of a core body of knowledge about human development, learning theory, language acquisition and disorders, and cultural and linguistic diversity, as well as relevant knowledge, skills, attitudes, value, and methods of associated disciplines. The purpose of this report is to identify the core competencies that the NJCLD believes are essential for both general and special educators who work with children with learning disabilities. The first part of the paper delineates competencies for general education teachers. The second part delineates additional competencies needed by special education teachers. Although these competencies represent the ideal, we believe they are worthy goals toward which every teacher preparation program should strive as it undergoes program review.

## General Education Teachers

*All prospective teachers need to have, at a minimum, an overview of the scope and sequence of the curriculum from kindergarten through 12th grade. In addition, teachers should be well prepared in their subject areas and understand the central concepts and tools of inquiry in these areas.*

The curricular areas required for all prospective teachers are reading, writing, communication skills, mathematics, social studies, the sciences, health/physical education, fine arts, and vocational/transition education. The emphasis in *early childhood* is on sensorimotor and social/emotional development, listening and speaking, and emerging reading, writing, and mathematical skills. In *elementary grades* the emphasis is on teaching and learning in reading, writing, and mathematics. During *middle school* the shift to classes by content area requires that children develop higher-level cognitive skills and understand the underlying concepts. Work on reading, writing, and reasoning within specific content areas throughout *middle and high school* is necessary. Also necessary is the integration of technology into all areas of instruction. Various professional organizations may assist in formulating specific knowledge and skill competencies for each of the content areas.

Although the majority of students with learning disabilities have specific difficulty in the area of reading, spelling, or writing, most of these students are placed in general education classrooms. Reading researchers have reached consensus that most reading and spelling disabilities originate with specific impairment of language processing. Therefore, in order to prevent problems in acquiring written language and to provide timely intervention for this major problem, general education teachers (especially in preschool and primary classrooms), special educators, speech-language pathologists, and other school-based personnel must have a thorough knowledge of the structure of oral and written language and its influence on literacy. In the content areas for which they are responsible and in other subjects, teachers must demonstrate proficiency in their spoken language, reading, and writing. *Teachers also must be competent to teach word analysis, spelling, reading comprehension, and the writing process.*

Students with learning disabilities also may have problems with mathematical calculations and reasoning. Therefore, general classroom teachers also must have a thorough knowledge and understanding of mathematical concepts and relationships and instructional techniques to assist such students in general education classrooms. Classroom mathematics instruction must be explicit and progress through three levels: concrete, representational, and abstract. Teachers and others who work with students who have learning disabilities need to determine how their students' learning differences affect their acquisition of knowledge. All prospective teachers should be taught how to individualize instruction and how to determine when and how to make accommodations and modifications.

## The Benefits of Collaboration

Collaboration among teaching professionals is a relatively new concept. With the current emphasis on mainstreaming (including students with disabilities in general education classrooms), general and special education teachers must work together cooperatively. General educators provide extensive knowledge in content areas; special educators and other specialists bring a variety of instructional techniques and knowledge that are especially beneficial to students with learning disabilities. Too often either the general or the special education teacher is relegated to an ancillary role. *Successful collaboration requires an equal partnership, willingness to collaborate, good communication skills, cooperation among the participating teachers, adequate planning time, and administrative support.*

Collaboration may include co-teaching situations in which special educators teach alongside their general education counterparts in the regular classroom. If this is the case, co-teachers may have to learn classroom management techniques and teaching strategies to accommodate their colleagues' teaching styles.

In teacher preparation programs general and special education professors should model collaboration by teaching classes together and designing integrated training programs. Professors involved in successful collaboration should serve as mentors for those entering teaching, those who provide related services, or experienced teachers who embark on new collaborative teaching experiences. Successful practitioners may assist in teaching students the fundamentals of collaborative teaching.

## Core Competencies

All graduates of teacher preparation programs need the following core competencies to help them work with students who have learning disabilities:

*Definitions and Characteristics*
- have knowledge of current definitions and characteristics of individuals with learning disabilities and how these disabilities affect students' development and educational performance

*Rights and Procedures*
- have knowledge of legal rights of the students and parents/guardians and the responsibilities of teachers and schools regarding special education and related services
- have knowledge of procedures for accessing and providing special education and related services (i.e., prereferral, referral, and implementation)

### Student Evaluation

- be familiar with commonly used instruments for assessment of students with learning disabilities
- identify informally each child's strengths and weaknesses across developmental areas
- use various formal and informal assessment techniques, including observation, interviews, samples of student work, student self-assessments, and teacher-made tests
- evaluate student performance on an ongoing basis in order to make instructional modifications and referrals when appropriate
- modify/adapt assessment tools in order to meet the specific needs of students with learning disabilities
- use grading procedures appropriate to the needs of students with learning disabilities

### Instruction

- develop and implement lesson plans to meet students' unique needs as identified in Individualized Education Programs (IEPs)
- demonstrate knowledge of the continuum of services and placements for students with learning disabilities
- plan and implement instruction in collaboration with the special education teacher when indicated
- modify instruction given students' unique learning characteristics
- modify instruction given such external factors as size of groupings, seating, pace of instruction, and noise level
- adapt technology for students with learning disabilities
- integrate students with learning disabilities into the academic and social classroom community

### Social/Emotional Development

- model respect and acceptance of students with learning disabilities
- provide opportunities for meaningful and ongoing social interactions among all students
- recognize and reinforce all student successes, even the small ones, to enhance self-esteem

### Classroom Management

- demonstrate various classroom management techniques that assist students with learning disabilities in their social interaction and self-regulation
- facilitate the participation of all students in large- and small-group interaction

### Relationships with Families and Colleagues

- promote positive attitudes toward individuals with disabilities and their families
- understand the child's culture and community
- develop an effective partnership with the family in the education of the child
- establish and maintain collegial relationships with school and community

## Special Education Teachers

Teachers planning to specialize in learning disabilities must have the core competencies required for general education teachers and an in-depth knowledge of the diverse nature of learning disabilities. A curriculum for preparing learning disabilities teachers should build on the competencies developed in the general education program (see above). To maximize learner outcomes, educators should have an opportunity to apply what they have learned in both supervised classroom settings and through carefully constructed classroom assignments. . . . Prospective teachers require ongoing practica and fieldwork to gain comprehensive experience in both general and special education. These practica should be supervised by master teachers and clinicians.

The NJCLD believes that educators who are earning degrees as learning disability specialists should have the following core competencies:

### Definitions and Characteristics

- demonstrate an understanding of the major theories, contributors, history, and trends in the field of learning disabilities
- demonstrate an understanding of (a) the characteristics of students with learning disabilities across the developmental spectrum, (b) cultural influences, (c) social/emotional development, and (d) medical interventions
- understand the differences between learning disabilities and other exceptionalities

### Rights and Procedures

- know federal, state, and local laws and regulations that directly affect students with learning disabilities
- understand and be able to discuss current legal and ethical issues in special education

### Student Evaluation

- evaluate the impact of related factors on a student's learning (e.g., self-regulatory behavior, social perception, social interaction)
- administer and interpret various assessment measures (e.g., formal and informal, achievement- and process-oriented instruments) to identify learning disabilities
- work on a multidisciplinary team to problem-solve and to determine prereferral interventions or eligibility for special education services
- understand the biases and limitations of assessment tools used to identify the abilities and disabilities of diverse learners
- identify and use alternative grading procedures (e.g., oral presentations, projects, portfolios)

### Instruction

- demonstrate competence in developing individualized education programs (IEPs) and working with multidisciplinary team to translate diagnostic data into interventions

- determine prereferral intervention strategies for students suspected of having learning disabilities
- match the unique needs of these students with mandated services along the continuum
- demonstrate the ability to use various specialized methods and materials (e.g., multisensory approaches)
- use assistive technology in instruction across the curriculum
- recommend to general educators appropriate academic modifications and accommodations (e.g., extended time on exams, alternative test formats, spell checkers, audiotaped instructional materials)
- provide instruction in life skills and preparation for transitions from elementary to middle school, middle to high school, and high school to adult living
- provide instruction in learning strategies (e.g., self-monitoring) and organizational strategies (e.g., note-taking, time management, study skills)

*Social/Emotional Development*

- understand the psychosocial variables affecting self-esteem, behavior, and academic progress
- understand the impact of the complexities and pervasive psychological effects of learning disabilities
- teach students self-awareness (e.g., understanding one's strengths and weaknesses), self-determination (e.g., goal-setting, decision-making and problem-solving), and self-advocacy
- teach students social skills to enhance social competence in school, outside school, and in work settings

*Classroom Management*

- collaborate with the general education teacher to assist in differentiating between primary behavior problems and those secondary to the learning disability
- develop and implement strategies to help students manage and regulate their behaviors in school

*Relationships with Families and Colleagues*

- provide effective resource assistance to and/or collaborate with general education teachers
- be involved with various parent and professional organizations and advocate for individuals with disabilities
- be able to collaborate with families to meet the child's special needs in the home
- collaborate and consult with related service providers, administrators, community services agencies, and others in planning for further education, careers, and transition/vocational programming

## Crucial Knowledge

The NJCLD believes that comprehensive interdisciplinary education programs are necessary for the preparation of all education professionals. To serve the needs of students with learning disabilities most effectively, all preservice teachers should have preparation that includes the competencies described in this paper. Furthermore, professionals who specialize in learning disabilities must have had additional experiences to demonstrate proficiency in all competencies described in this report.

# EFFECTIVE LEARNING STRATEGIES FOR STUDENTS WITH LEARNING DISABILITIES

David A. Sousa

Students with learning disabilities typically have problems organizing information, following directions, performing tasks in sequence, and memorizing material, explains David A. Sousa in the following excerpt from his book *How the Special Needs Brain Learns*. However, Sousa maintains, these students can achieve considerable success by the use of specific learning strategies designed to help them overcome such problems. He defines learning strategies as efficient and orderly procedures that people employ when learning, remembering, or performing; examples include taking notes, making an outline, and looking for errors in one's own schoolwork. The author presents detailed steps that educators can follow in teaching students with learning disabilities how to use these strategies. An international educational consultant, Sousa has extensive teaching experience from elementary school to the college level and is the author of numerous articles and books.

An analysis of almost 30 years of research indicates that the following interventions are most effective with learning disabled students:
- The most effective form of teaching was one that combined direct instruction (e.g., teacher-directed lecture, discussion, and learning from textbooks) with teaching students the strategies of learning (e.g., memorization techniques, study skills).
- The component that had the greatest effect on student achievement was *control of task difficulty*, in which, for example, the teacher provided the necessary assistance or sequenced tasks from easy to difficult. Working in small groups (five or less) and using structured questioning were also highly effective.
- When groups of students with learning disabilities were exposed to strategy instruction (i.e., how to learn), their achievement was greater than that of groups exposed solely to direct instruction. . . .

What actually makes learning difficult for students with learning disabilities has been the subject of research for many years. Examining the challenges of these students yields clues about the way they interact with their environment and possible interventions that may help them be more successful. Neil Sturomski has proposed that learners will benefit from strategies to help them learn. This section presents some of the findings and suggestions he included in a 1997 article for the National Information Center for Children and Youth with Disabilities.

## What Is Learning?

Learning is an active process of acquiring and retaining knowledge so it can be applied in future situations. The ability to recall and apply new learning involves a complex interaction between the learner and the material being learned. Learning is likely to occur when a student has opportunities to practice the new information, receive feedback from the teacher, and apply the knowledge or skill in familiar and unfamiliar situations with less and less assistance from others.

Students bring to each new learning task a varied background of their own ideas, beliefs, opinions, attitudes, motivation, skills, and prior knowledge. They also bring the strategies and techniques they have learned in order to make learning more efficient. All these aspects contribute directly to students' ability to learn, and to remember and use what has been learned.

Teachers can facilitate a lifetime of successful learning by equipping students with a repertoire of strategies and tools for learning. These might include ways to organize oneself and new material; techniques to use while reading, writing, and studying mathematics or other subjects; and systematic steps to follow when working through a learning task or reflecting upon one's own learning.

*Learning Difficulties of Students with Learning Disabilities.* Sturomski stresses that students who have learning disabilities may have problems because they

- Are often overwhelmed, disorganized, and frustrated in new learning situations.
- Have difficulty following directions.
- Have trouble with the visual or auditory perception of information.
- Have problems performing school tasks, such as writing compositions, taking notes, doing written homework, or taking paper-and-pencil tests.
- Have a history of academic problems. Such students may believe that they cannot learn, that school tasks are just too difficult and not worth the effort, or that, if they do succeed at a task, it must have been due to luck.
- Do not readily believe that there is a connection between what

they do, the effort they make, and the likelihood of academic success. These negative beliefs about their ability to learn, and the nature of learning itself, can lower self-esteem and have far-reaching academic consequences.

## Coping with the Difficulties

Acquiring the necessary knowledge, skills, and strategies for functioning independently in our society is as important to students with learning disabilities as it is to their peers without disabilities. Perhaps one of the most fundamental skills for everyone to learn is *how to learn*. Students can become effective, lifelong learners when they master certain techniques and strategies to assist learning and know which techniques are useful in different kinds of learning situations.

We all use various methods and strategies to help us remember new information or skills. Yet, some of us are more conscious of our own learning processes than others. For instance, many students know little about the learning process, their own strengths and weaknesses in a learning situation, and what strategies and techniques they naturally tend to use when learning something new.

Hence, students with learning disabilities need to become strategic learners, and not haphazardly use whatever strategies or techniques they have developed on their own. To be able to decide which strategies to use, for example, students need to observe how others think or act when using various strategies. Learning skills develop when students receive opportunities to discuss, reflect upon, and practice personal strategies with classroom materials and appropriate skills. Through feedback, teachers help students refine new strategies and monitor their choices. Over time, teachers can diminish active guidance as students assume more responsibility for their own strategic learning.

## What Are Learning Strategies?

Learning strategies are efficient, effective, and organized steps or procedures used when learning, remembering, or performing. These tools and techniques help us to understand and to retain new material or skills, to integrate this new information with what we already know in a way that makes sense, and to recall the information or skill later. When we are trying to learn new information or perform a task, our strategies include both cognitive and behavioral aspects.

Strategies can be simple or complex. Simple learning strategies are cognitive activities usually associated with less challenging learning tasks. Some examples of simple strategies are the following:

- Taking notes
- Making a chart or outline
- Asking the teacher questions
- Asking ourselves questions
- Using resource books or the Internet

- Re-reading what we don't understand
- Asking someone to check our work
- Developing a mnemonic device

Complex strategies help us accomplish more complex tasks involving multiple steps or higher-order thinking, such as analysis or answering "What if . . . ?" questions. The following are examples of complex strategies:

- Planning, writing, and revising an essay
- Identifying sources of information
- Stating main ideas and supporting our position
- Distinguishing fact from opinion
- Searching for and correcting errors in our work
- Keeping track of our progress
- Being aware of our thought processes
- Evaluating the validity of sources

The research literature is full of suggestions for strategy interventions designed to make learners more aware of what they are doing.

## Types of Learning Strategies

Sturomski also notes the different ways learning strategies can be categorized. One way, for example, is to classify strategies as either cognitive or metacognitive.

*Cognitive Strategies.* These help a person process and manipulate information to perform tasks such as taking notes, asking questions, or filling out a chart. They tend to be task specific, that is, certain cognitive strategies are useful when learning or performing certain tasks.

*Metacognitive Strategies.* These are more executive in nature and are used when planning, monitoring, and evaluating learning or strategy performance. They are often referred to as self-regulatory strategies, helping students become aware of learning as a process and of what actions will facilitate that process. For example, taking the time to plan before writing assists students in writing a good composition. The ability to evaluate one's work, the effectiveness of learning, or even the use of a strategy is also metacognitive, demonstrating that a learner is aware of and thinking about how learning occurs.

Students who use metacognitive strategies frequently tend to become self-regulated learners. They set goals for learning, coach themselves in positive ways, and use self-instruction to guide themselves through learning problems. Further, they monitor their comprehension or progress and reward themselves for success. Just as students can be taught cognitive, task-specific strategies, so can they be taught self-regulatory, metacognitive ones. In fact, the most effective interventions combine the use of cognitive and metacognitive strategies.

Strategies have also been categorized by their purpose or function for the learner. B.K. Lenz, E.S. Ellis, and D. Scanlon suggest three types of functional strategies:

1. Acquisition strategy: Used initially to learn new information or skills
2. Storage strategy: Used to manipulate or transform information so that it can effectively be placed in memory
3. Knowledge strategy: Used to recall or to show what has been learned

## Research About Learning Strategies

Research into strategies of learning has been going on for over 30 years, long before the availability of brain scanning technologies. Since the 1970s, researchers at the University of Kansas have investigated the benefits of strategy instruction, especially for individuals with learning disabilities. Their work produced one of the most well researched and well articulated models for teaching students to use learning strategies. Known as the Strategies Integration Model, or SIM, this method outlines a series of steps so that educators can effectively teach any number of strategies or strategic approaches.

Recent cognitive research supports the notion that learning and retention are more likely to occur when students can observe, engage in, discuss, reflect upon, and practice the new learning. When teachers help students to use learning strategies and to generalize their strategic knowledge to other academic and nonacademic situations, they are promoting student independence in the process of learning.

## Using the Strategies

For students who have learning disabilities, learning strategy instruction holds great educational promise for the following reasons:

- Instruction helps students learn how to learn and become more effective in the successful performance of academic, social, or job-related tasks. Students can better deal with immediate academic demands as well as cope with similar tasks in different settings under different conditions throughout life. The strategies are particularly powerful in the face of new learning situations.
- Instruction makes students aware of how strategies work, why they work, when they work, and where they can be used. To assist students, teachers will need to
  - talk about strategies explicitly,
  - name and describe each strategy,
  - model how each strategy is used by thinking aloud while performing tasks relevant to students,
  - provide students with multiple opportunities to use the strategies with a variety of materials, and
  - provide feedback and guidance while students refine and internalize the use of each strategy.

Ultimately, responsibility for strategy use needs to shift from teachers to students. This promotes independent learners with the cognitive flexibility necessary to address the many learning challenges they will encounter in their lives.

Although no single technique or intervention can address all the varied needs of students with learning disabilities, teaching the strategies of learning will help these students become better equipped to face current and future learning tasks. By learning how to learn, they can become independent, lifelong learners—one of the primary goals of education.

Students with learning disabilities often have negative feelings about learning and about themselves. Because of past experiences, these students believe they cannot learn or that the work is simply too difficult. As a result, they may believe they cannot achieve success in learning through their own efforts. Teachers need to address this issue when presenting information on the strategies of learning. By modeling positive self-statements, teachers can convince students to attribute success in learning to their own efforts and to the use of appropriate learning strategies. For learning strategies to be successful, students need to have a positive self-image and recognize the connection between effort and success. . . .

## The Strategies Integration Model

Much has been learned through research regarding effective learning-strategy instruction. As mentioned earlier, a well-articulated instructional approach known as the Strategies Integration Model (SIM) has emerged from research conducted at the University of Kansas. Based on cognitive behavior modification, the SIM is one of the field's most comprehensive tools for providing strategy instruction. It can be used to teach virtually any strategic intervention.

First, the teacher selects a strategy that is clearly linked to the tasks students need to perform at the place they need to perform them. When the strategy is matched to student needs, they perceive relevancy and tend to be motivated to learn and use the strategy. After selecting the strategy or approach to teach, the six steps of the SIM guide the actual instruction.

*Step 1. Determine Prior Knowledge and Generate Interest in Learning the Strategy.* It is important to use a type of pretest to determine how much students already know about using the strategy. This information provides a starting point for instruction. Younger students, for example, may have no understanding of how they learn; older students may have already encountered their learning weaknesses. Motivate students by letting them know that gains in learning can occur when the strategy is used effectively. Studies have shown that it is important to tell students directly that learning this strategy using effort and persistence will help them achieve whatever skill is being addressed.

Use a pretest that centers on the materials and tasks that students actually encounter in class. Following the pretest, the class should discuss the results by asking questions such as:

- How did we do?
- Were we able to perform the task successfully?
- What types of errors did we make? Why?
- What did we do, or think about, to help ourselves while taking the pretest?
- What difficulties did we have? How did we address those difficulties?

If students did not perform particularly well, then discuss a strategy or technique that will help them perform that task more successfully in the future.

According to the SIM, it is important to obtain a commitment from students to learn the strategy. To accomplish this, teachers can discuss the value of the strategy and the fact that they are committed to helping the students. Teachers should point out the likelihood that success may not be immediate, but that success will come if the student perseveres and practices the strategy.

Student-teacher collaboration in use of the strategy is especially important with elementary school students. Teachers need to discuss and practice strategies with these young students frequently. The commitments can be verbal or in writing, but the idea here is to get the students involved and to make them aware that their participation in learning and in using the strategy is vital to their eventual success.

*Step 2. Describe the Strategy.* In this step, teachers clearly define the strategy, give examples, discuss the benefits of learning the strategy, and ask students to determine various ways the strategy can be used. The teacher should also identify real-life assignments in specific classes in which students can apply the strategy and ask students if they can think of other work for which the strategy might be useful. Students should also be told the various stages involved in learning the strategy, so they know what to expect.

After this overview, the students are ready to delve more deeply into hearing about and using the strategy. Instruction becomes more specific so that each step of the strategy is described in detail and presented in such a way that students can easily remember it. Acronyms can help students remember the various steps involved.

Displaying a poster or chart about the strategy and its steps will also help memory and retention. During this phase, the class also discusses how this new approach to a specific task differs from what students are currently using. For closure, conclude with a review of what has been learned.

*Step 3. Model the Strategy.* Modeling the strategy is an essential component of strategy instruction. In this step, teachers overtly use the strategy to help students perform a relevant classroom or authentic task, talking aloud as they work so that students can observe how a person thinks and what a person does while using the strategy. For example, you could model

- deciding which strategy to use to perform the task at hand;
- working through the task using that strategy;
- monitoring performance (i.e., is the strategy being applied correctly, and is it helping the learner effectively complete the work?);
- revising one's strategic approach; and,
- making positive self-statements.

The self-talk that the teacher provides as a model can become a powerful guide for students as responsibility for using the strategy transfers to them.

*Step 4. Practice the Strategy.* Practice leads to retention. The more students and teachers collaborate to use the strategy, the more likely the strategy will become part of the students' strategic repertoire. Initial guided practice is designed to check for understanding and first applications.

Students should be encouraged to think aloud as they work through their practice tasks, explaining the problems they are having, the decisions they are making, or the physical actions they are taking. These student "think alouds" should increasingly reveal the specific strategy being used to help them complete the task successfully. Initially, the "think alouds" should be part of teacher-directed instruction. Later, the students benefit greatly from practicing in small groups, where they listen and help each other understand the task, why the strategy might be useful in completing the task, and how to apply the strategy to the task. Eventually, the practice sessions become self-mediated as students work independently to complete tasks while using the strategy.

As practice continues, the level of difficulty of the materials being used should gradually increase. In the beginning, students practice using the strategy with materials that are at or slightly below their comfort level, so they do not become frustrated by overly difficult content. The materials must be well matched to the strategy so that students can readily understand the strategy's value. As students become more proficient in using the strategy, introduce materials that are more difficult.

## Practical Aspects

*Step 5. Provide Feedback.* The feedback that teachers give students on their use of the strategy is a critical component of the SIM. It helps students learn how to use a strategy effectively and how to change what they are doing when a particular approach is unsuccessful. It is also important for students to reflect upon their approach to and completion of the task and to self-correct when necessary. What aspects of the task did they complete well? What aspects were hard? Did any problems arise, and what did they do to solve the problems?

What might they do differently the next time they have to complete a similar task?

*Step 6. Promote Application to Other Tasks (Generalization).* The value of using learning strategies increases greatly when students are able to apply the strategy in new situations. It may not become obvious to many students that the strategy they have been learning and practicing may be ideal for helping them to complete a learning task in a different classroom or learning situation; this is particularly true of students with learning disabilities. Thus, merely exposing the students to strategy training is not sufficient for both strategy learning and strategy utilization to occur. Guided and consistent practice in generalizing how the strategies can transfer to various settings and tasks is vital for students with learning disabilities, as are repeated reminders that strategies of learning can be used in new situations.

Therefore, teachers need to discuss with students what transfer is all about and how and when students might use the strategy in other settings. An important part of this discussion will be getting students to review the actual work that they have in other classes and discussing with students how the strategy might be useful in completing that work. Actually going through the steps of the strategy with specific work assignments can be very effective.

Students can generate their own examples of contexts in which to apply the strategy, such as homework assignments, job applications, friendly letters, English papers, written problems in mathematics, and spelling practice. Additionally, teachers within a school may wish to coordinate among themselves to promote student use of strategies across settings, so that the strategies being taught in one classroom are mentioned and supported by other teachers as well. All of these approaches will promote student generalization of the strategy.

# IMPROVING EARLY INTERVENTION FOR READING DISABILITIES

Robert Pasternack

Robert Pasternack is the assistant secretary for special education and rehabilitative services for the U.S. Department of Education. The following selection is taken from a statement Pasternack delivered to the U.S. House of Representatives subcommittee on educational reform on June 6, 2002, at a hearing on learning disabilities. While he acknowledges that learning disabilities are varied, Pasternack focuses on reading skills, which he considers to be the major foundation for school learning. Reading difficulties are common among school-age children, he explains, many of whom are not identified as having a learning disability. Pasternack stresses the importance of using new scientific knowledge on the nature of reading and language acquisition to develop appropriate instruction techniques for students who have reading disabilities.

Mr. Chairman, members of the committee, I want to thank you for the opportunity to appear before you today to discuss issues relating to learning disabilities. As you are no doubt aware, the Individuals with Disabilities Education Act (IDEA) defines a learning disability as a "disorder in one or more of the basic psychological processes involved in understanding or in using spoken or written language, which may manifest itself in an imperfect ability to listen, think, speak, read, write, spell, or to do mathematical calculations." Learning disability is not a single disorder and the various types of disabilities frequently co-occur with one another and with social skill deficits and emotional behavioral disorders. In addition, these problems may mildly, moderately, or severely impair the learning process. We know that children identified as having specific learning disabilities may have problems that affect many areas of learning. However, I want to focus my remarks today on the area of reading. The development of reading skills serves as the major foundational academic ability for all school-based learning.

Our research at the Office of Special Education and Rehabilitative Services (OSERS) and the Office of Educational Research and Improve-

Robert Pasternack, address to the U.S. House of Representatives, Education and the Workforce Subcommittee on Education Reform, June 6, 2002.

ment (OERI) and the research at the National Institute of Child Health and Development (NICHD) has consistently shown that if children do not learn to understand and use language, to read and write, to calculate and reason mathematically, to solve problems, and to communicate their ideas and perspectives, their opportunities for a fulfilling and rewarding life are seriously compromised.

Specifically, we have learned that school failure has devastating consequences with respect to self-esteem, social development, and opportunities for advanced education and meaningful employment. Nowhere are these consequences of academic failure more apparent than when children fail to learn to read. The development of reading skills serves as the major foundational academic ability for all school-based learning. Without the ability to read, the opportunities for academic and occupational success are limited.

The President [George W. Bush] and the Congress have clearly recognized the pivotal importance of reading in the No Child Left Behind (NCLB) Act, and in particular the Reading First and Early Reading First initiatives supported through NCLB. The NCLB requires that States and school districts focus on reading through the development of scientifically based programs, strategies, and materials that will help ensure that all children learn to read. And just as importantly, the law holds States and school districts accountable for achieving results. This strong emphasis on reading is intended to get schools to use scientifically based reading instruction that incorporates what we know about what works in the teaching of reading— things like phonemic awareness, phonics, fluency, vocabulary, and reading comprehension.

## The Scope of the Problem

It is clear from research conducted by OSERS and the NICHD that reading failure affects children earlier and more intensely than we previously thought. By the end of the first grade, children displaying difficulty learning to read begin to feel less positive about themselves than when they started school. In later years, these children experience even further decline in self-esteem and motivation. The consequences are dire.

According to the National Center for Education Statistics (NCES, 2000), thirty-seven percent of fourth graders nationally cannot read at a basic level. They cannot read and understand a short paragraph of the type one would find in a simple children's book. For children living in poverty, these statistics are even worse. In many low-income urban school districts the percentage of students in the fourth grade who cannot read at a basic level approaches seventy percent. Nearly half of the 6.5 million children with disabilities receiving special education are identified as having a specific learning disability. Of the 2.8 million children with a specific learning disability, approximately 80 percent to 90 percent have their primary difficulties in learning to read. Of the children who will eventually drop out of school, over seventy-five percent will report difficulties in learning to read. Surveys of adolescents and young adults with criminal records indicate that many have reading difficulties. Approximately half of children and adolescents with a history of substance abuse have reading problems. Needless to say, the inability of many of our nation's children to develop basic reading skills is not just an education problem, it is a national social and health problem as well.

## Reading Problems and Special Education

While reading is important for all children, it is especially important for children with disabilities. Most of the available information and research on learning disabilities is in the area of reading difficulties. This information has been extremely valuable in our understanding of reading difficulties.

Recent OSERS and NICHD-funded research indicates that many children with deficits in the area of reading can learn to read at "nearly normal" levels when scientifically based reading instruction is used. However, we also know that some children with reading related learning disabilities do not significantly improve their reading skills even when provided scientifically based classroom instruction by highly qualified and highly trained personnel. We do not fully understand what conditions need to be in place to remediate the severe intractable reading difficulties of these children. However, we do know that these children will require specially designed instruction delivered through the IDEA.

## Important Interventions

Providing the appropriate supports to children who learn to read with varying degrees of ease requires understanding the range of reading difficulties and the concomitant range of interventions needed to serve all children. Primary prevention involves universal assessment and instruction, such as research-based schoolwide reading programs, to avert the onset of reading deficits and identify those at risk of failing to learn to read and providing early intervention to those that need it. Secondary prevention refers to scientifically based strategies and procedures that quickly improve reading skills while they are still emerging. For example, services provided through Title I of the ESEA [Elementary and Secondary Education Act] and other compensatory or supplemental education programs are secondary interventions. Both primary and secondary interventions can include working with small groups of students who need additional support or assistance to successfully acquire skills in reading. The final level of intervention, the tertiary level, involves providing more intense, scientifically based specialized instruction, such as one-on-one interventions for individual students.

Additional research is needed, however, to identify interventions that will be effective in helping those children with intractable reading problems. Without such research, approximately six percent of all children, those with the most severe reading difficulties, may never gain the skills or opportunity necessary to achieve proficiency. This research must also help us differentiate those children with reading problems who are instructional casualties, children who could learn to read if provided with the appropriate scientifically based instruction, from those with actual specific learning disabilities. The remaining children, those who do not respond to the scientifically based interventions we have identified so far, are the right children to bring into special education. One significant challenge is to ensure that we help schools make these differentiations and to conduct research that will identify the right interventions to use with the right children to achieve the right result.

## Necessary Steps

In order to improve results for children with learning disabilities, we must be willing to challenge the past and build on what we know. We must take the necessary steps to increase our knowledge base and implement scientifically based best practices.

First, we must build on the principles embodied in the NCLB Act. Specifically, we must focus on accountability for achieving results for all children including children with disabilities. Also in line with the principles of NCLB, we must focus our efforts on disseminating what works. We must identify and share best practices and not be afraid to discard those that do not yield the results that our children deserve.

Second, we will never help children with disabilities, especially those with learning disabilities, by focusing only on those who are in special education. It is important to understand that many children, including many who are not in special education, have difficulty in learning to read. This is clearly an area where what benefits children with disabilities will benefit all children who have difficulty learning how to read.

Third, we must be adamant about our goal to use scientifically based instruction and ensure that it is provided only by highly trained and qualified teachers and other paraprofessionals. As you will hear from others asked to testify here today, so much more is being learned from the scientific community than we have ever known about the nature of reading and language acquisition. We need to continue to draw on that knowledge, and promote the development of new knowledge through careful targeting of research resources, partnering with other organizations like NICHD, and, finally, disseminating what we learn.

## Increasing Efforts

Fourth, now that we have the tools to help many children who have difficulty in reading, both those who are identified as learning disabled and those who are not, we must increase our efforts to help those children who are considered to have intractable reading difficulties. These are the children who without question need the benefits of IDEA-supported programs.

Fifth, as we think about the use of existing research and the need for future research, we must stress the importance of collaboration in research and in practice. Like research in so many other fields, those of us who are concerned about serving children with disabilities must reach out to the scientific community, the medical community, and others whose work can inform and improve ours. We need to continue to leverage our resources to partner with entities such as NICHD and others. While we have done that in the past and are doing so now, I believe that we must increase our collaborative efforts in research and best practices.

Finally, we must specifically focus attention on methods and strategies for prevention, early identification and early intervention. We need to identify and serve children sooner who need reading and other learning interventions. We know that effective early interventions work. The more children that we can reach early with effective interventions, especially in the area of reading, the more we will be able to help and, in some cases, reduce or even eliminate the need for future special education services. We must also develop solid prevention models that will keep many children from ever needing reading remediation. Helping children with a range of reading difficulties early will help us to focus intensively on those students who do not respond to early interventions.

## The Push for More

I firmly believe that the provision of effective services to the children in special education who have learning disabilities is a high priority. We must indeed do more, not just because children with learning disabilities comprise such a large percentage of all disabled children, but we can do more. The convergence of scientific research about LD, especially reading difficulties associated with LD, has placed us on the edge of new knowledge that we did not have even a few short years ago. We now know, for example, that the way we have traditionally looked at assessment of learning disabilities needs to be re-thought based on recent research in the use and role of IQ tests in assessments for eligibility. We know that using IQ discrepancy between the test and performance is not always an indicator of a learning disability. Indeed, some research indicates that if a child who reads slowly has IQ scores that are above average, that child might receive services under the IDEA based on the discrepancy between the IQ scores and the reading ability. On the other hand, another child who also reads slowly but has IQ scores that are average may not receive any services because of the lack of a significant discrepancy. Such approaches to assessment may clearly result in some children who need services not getting them while others who do not need them will receive them.

We have much to do in serving the 2.8 million children with learning disabilities. There is clearly a need for continued research and clearly a need for us to better use the research that we already have. We must look for results, not promises in what we do. I look forward to working with you, Mr. Chairman, and other members of this committee as we move forward in improving the lives of all children through the IDEA.

# Providing Order and Focus Through the Arts

Sally L. Smith

Sally L. Smith is an education professor at American University in Washington, D.C. She is also the founder and director of The Lab School of Washington, an innovative school for students with learning disabilities that emphasizes hands-on experiential education and the use of the arts to teach academic skills. In the following excerpt from her book *The Power of the Arts: Creative Strategies for Teaching Exceptional Learners*, Smith describes how an educational program centered on the arts can help children with learning disabilities to become more organized and focused. Students with learning disabilities have difficulties understanding information as imparted by regular instruction in a standard classroom, she observes; however, they often respond well to creative instructional techniques involving crafts projects, artwork, theater, music, and dance.

My experience with my son who had learning disabilities showed me that he was thoroughly disorganized: He had difficulty focusing; could understand material presented verbally but could not repeat it back in rote fashion; and could not remember names, titles of books or movies, or supposedly simple things such as addresses and telephone numbers. Anything involving sequences such as the alphabet, numbers in order, and the days of the week, months of the year, and the seasons eluded him. I soon discovered that there were a whole host of youngsters just like my son who had the same basic problems.

When my son learned in first grade about a Navajo rain dance, his hand shot up and he compared the Navajo rain dance to Greek myths. "People have to believe in these," he said. "Maybe, also, they thought they could bring about what they wanted to have happen by doing a dance or telling a story." His first-grade teacher went up to him, shook him hard, and said, "If you know all that, why can't you read the word *cat?*" The teacher may not have realized that reading uses a different part of the brain than comparing and reasoning; however, her frustration with students like my son was very common.

Students with learning disabilities often make very astute remarks; therefore, their teachers and, sometimes, their parents cannot understand why the students have difficulty with tasks that other students perform with ease. Parents and teachers decide that the students are lazy and that they *could* read if they only *would*. My son, the same 6-year-old who had remarked so intelligently in class, hid in the bathroom or under a table during reading time. He had been able to fake reading by using picture or context clues and making inferences, but when he was faced with the barren desert of letters placed together to form a word, he ran away, claiming to have bladder trouble—one malady he did not have.

There were incredible inconsistencies between my son's advanced vocabulary, excellent reasoning, and vibrant imagination and his inability to see the difference between a straight line and an angle. He did not know that 2 plus 2 equals 4 and was not even sure whether 4 was more than or less than 2. Erratic, uneven, and unpredictable, a jumble of "can dos" and "cannot dos," traditional schooling did not work for my son.

Facts did not stick in my son's mind. However, we found that he responded with alacrity to highly dramatic stories read aloud and to stories with pictures that he could act out and then discuss. Although he was very clumsy with his hands, he enjoyed working on very big short-term projects. He loved having a project to take to his room or to take home. Drumbeats and steady hand clapping helped him get organized. This profile was similar to a number of students enrolled at The Lab School. Many other students at the school were extremely talented with their hands but had very little language with which to express themselves.

## Learning by Doing

Children with learning disabilities and attention-deficit/hyperactivity disorder (ADHD) experience neurologically based disorganization. The child with learning disabilities usually has difficulty beginning a project because he does not know how to break it down into meaningful chunks: first, next, and last. This is true in the arts as well as in the classroom. These children do not have the organizational skills necessary for learning.

Young children understand touch, gesture, rhythm, tone, and movement before they understand words. They babble, croon, and sing before they speak. They color, draw, and paint before they form letters. They dance and leap and act out stories before they can read. Young children use the arts—pretending, constructing, dancing, and doing—to make sense of their environment.

As a young child learns from doing, a child who is neurologically immature must be given the same opportunities before she can handle abstractions. What happens first, next, and last is crucial in a woodworking or crafts project as well as in drama or dance. The same neurological organization is necessary for reading—for looking at the beginning, middle, and end of a word, phrase, or sentence.

Through each of the art forms, a child can learn to distinguish colors, shapes, forms, and sounds; discrimination through the use of the child's hands, body, eyes, ears, and senses is part of the artistic experience. Learning to look and to listen and remembering what has been seen and heard—problem areas for students with learning disabilities—are emphasized in the arts. The arts help children organize experiences. They help make sense of the world and the messages that come in through the senses. The arts can help students with learning disablilities develop and strengthen the perceptual skills that form the foundation for further learning.

Discipline underlies every artistic endeavor. There is an order—a progression of steps—to every creation. People think of the arts as being very free; they are, but they only become so after one has mastered a set of basic skills. The student with learning disabilities or ADHD, who is consumed by indiscriminate attention and overreactiveness, needs experiences that have a clear beginning, middle, and end. Understanding sequences is vital for the child who can talk to you about [the Greek poet] Homer or gravity but cannot tell you the order of the days of the week or the seasons, count to 20, or say the alphabet in the proper sequence. What happens first, next, and last is as crucial in a painting or crafts project as it is in drama or dance. Organizing oneself is mandatory.

Most exceptional learners can learn very sophisticated material as long as the teacher thoroughly understands it, breaks it down into simple parts, and teaches it step by step. Very elementary skills that are ordinarily introduced to much younger children can be presented to older children with learning disabilities in a sophisticated way so as to lure them into mastering these skills. When a group of 10-year-olds needed the experience of touching and discriminating among textures, a typical nursery school experience, The Lab School of Washington set up a "tactile museum" that included a wide variety of materials for touching, including Styrofoam, sponge, velvet, fur, and metal. Because no other school had a tactile museum, the students who set up the museum were very proud of their accomplishment and felt they were performing an adult activity; at the same time, their teachers were able to give them the exact experience they needed. The arts lend themselves to the imaginative use of concrete materials and experiences to teach organizational skills.

## Establishing Order in Space and Time

When structure is provided from the outside, children who experience disorganization are set free and given the safety to learn. Establishing a time, a space, and a place for all things is the key. This is why the woodwork shop has a pegboard with tools hanging from it, each one fitting into the thick shape of its outline. For the student who has little understanding of his body in space, there is a big masking-tape square labeled "your space" in front of a woodworking table. There are children who have no concept of their own parameters or borders; therefore, teachers have to be guided to design the arts in a way to put boundaries around the children. For many, photography and videography—looking through a camera to frame and focus—provide the necessary structure.

The arts can help build organizational skills, which can further the process of neural maturation. Too often, children who are failing in academics are placed in clinical settings or schools where they are given more academics—more attention to the reading, writing, and arithmetic they cannot do. Increasing the workload does not help, and at the same time, these children lose the opportunity to have experiences in which they can feel competent or can learn facts to build huge storehouses of information.

Students work as hard in the arts as they do in traditional classrooms; the work is just different. When doing collages, some students cannot see the difference between the foreground and the background. Collages can be used to teach just that. These are special problems, and they often arise in printmaking as well. Printmaking can be taught so that a child must print left to right and look for and recreate patterns. At The Lab School, we used potato prints to sequence a mammoth hunt. One student sequenced them perfectly, but all backwards.

Typical in exceptional learners is a lack of a sense of time. For example, the only way 8-year-old Eric understood the concept of a short amount of time was when his mother explained that the time it takes to eat one bowl of cereal is a short time, and the time it takes to eat ten bowls of cereal is a long time. In art class, Eric would begin working when three-quarters of the class was over, and then he didn't want to leave when the class ended. The teacher/artist who taught Eric found a special place for him to sit and left a picture schedule at his desk for him to study each day. The picture schedule showed Eric going to get paper, then finding his paints, and finally painting a picture. After a few months, Eric was able to draw his own schedules and manage his time better, despite the fact that his internal clock was still not working properly.

## Discovering Relationships, Sequence, and Logic

In addition to having difficulties with organization and focus, many exceptional learners experience difficulty with abstract concepts and social relationships. They may not be able to link cause and effect and often have trouble understanding relationships between people, predicting the consequences of their own behavior on others, and understanding the relationship of one set of behaviors to a broader pattern of behaviors.

Just as young children use only what is directly in front of them to learn and to grow, children who have neurological delays understand and learn best from direct interaction with materials and objects. Concrete materials allow them to discover relationships, draw inferences, and make abstractions on their own. Often such experiential learning is the only way these children can begin to grasp abstract concepts and higher thinking operations.

Consider the learning styles of Bennett, age 8, and Rick, age 10. Bennett understands such concepts as truth, honesty, equality, and integrity just from hearing about these concepts from his parents and teachers and from books he reads. Rick does not. Rick understands these concepts only through playing games, playing with objects, role playing, looking at pictures, watching videos, and participating in discussions. For example, when Rick's teachers were trying to explain to Rick the concept of truth, they asked him to fold a piece of paper into three equal parts. Rick saw that Harry and Carolyn each folded their papers differently from the way he folded his, but they still ended up with three equal parts. Using this model, Rick was taught that despite the fact that [the ancient Greek philosophers] Socrates, Plato, and Aristotle all had different theories, they were the same in that they all were seeking the truth. Although Bennett enjoys learning about these three philosophers in this way, he does not *need* this approach to understand the concept. Rick cannot understand the concept unless he is taught experientially.

When working with children with learning disabilities, it is important to keep in mind each child's particular experience and to create an environment in which the child may learn from further experiences. Given a structured environment and materials that will prompt the discovery of relationships, nuances, and concepts, children with learning disabilities can bridge the gulf between the world of literal meanings and the world of the abstract. The child, however, cannot be told how to bridge the gulf; he has to bridge it on his own. Teachers have to provide alluring, enticing materials that will attract his attention and excite him into making connections and discovering relationships.

## Theoretical Underpinnings

My design for the heavy use of all the art forms has been greatly influenced by the works of the Swiss psychologist Jean Piaget and the American educational theorist John Dewey. To some extent, the work of American psychologist Jerome Bruner influenced me, and I find that American educator Howard Gardner's theory of multiple intelligences confirms the work I have done since 1966.

Jean Piaget identified four stages of intellectual development in children, each stage dependent upon the preceding stage. Children can reach these stages at different ages depending on their particular rate of development. Piaget called the first stage, during which the child organizes his world through movement and sensation (typically occurring between birth and age 2 years), the *sensorimotor* stage. During the second stage, the *preoperational* stage (typically occurring between the ages of 2 and 7), a child's mental life is dominated by what *seems* to be rather than what logically must be. During the third stage, the *concrete operational* stage (typically occurring between the ages of 7 and 11), the child's thoughts are still limited to concrete experiences and cannot deal with abstractions until they are represented concretely. During the fourth stage, the *formal operations* phase (typically occurring from age 11 and up), a child can perform logical operations without objects, can infer, and can make generalizations and deductions. Piaget's four stages illustrate that educators need to teach children at their developmental levels while using materials appropriate to their chronological ages (the number of years lived). When the development of the central nervous system is delayed, a child remains in the concrete stages for a much longer period of time and must be taught concretely no matter how old she is. The child needs experience with materials to know them well. Although teaching at a higher level may seem to be age-appropriate for this child, it is an exercise in futility; perhaps this is why they clamor to see something, to touch it, to experiment with it, and to do it.

> *Even though 12-year-old Mark looks like a typical 12-year-old and has an impressive vocabulary, he is developmentally more similar to a child between the ages of 7 and 11. Thus, he needs to be taught in concrete ways. In learning the months of the year, Mark had to be taught through 12 boxes, each box illustrated as the month with four or five smaller boxes inside them serving as weeks and seven cards inside those serving as days. Coloring the boxes with, for example, scenes of January and holidays such as New Year's Day and Martin Luther King Day helped Mark understand the concept.*

At the end of the 20th century, education experts began to see the value of teaching according to a child's developmental rather than chronological age. A 1997 article in *Newsweek* by B. Kantrowitz and P. Wingert pointed out that a growing number of educators are beginning to recognize that children learn best through active, hands-on teaching methods such as games and dramatic play and that because children develop at varying rates, schools have to allow for these differences.

## Educational Inquiries

Dewey, an early advocate of experiential education wrote, "Anything which can be called a study, whether arithmetic, history, geography or one of the natural sciences, must be derived from the materials which at the outset fall within the scope of ordinary life experience." Dewey felt that, too often, education was imposed from above, with adult standards and inappropriate subject matter beyond the reach of experience of the young learner. He pleaded with educators to let children learn by doing. Immersed in the learning process and with appropriate materials to accomplish the purpose, children discover relationships, make connections, and draw conclusions. It is important that the teacher have a clear purpose or objective so that the provided materials will lead the child into inquiry. Dewey was a great proponent of the use of the arts. In his book, *The Schooled Society*, he said, "And so the expressive impulse of the children, the art instinct, grows out of the communicating and constructive instincts. . . . Make the construction adequate, make it full, free, and flexible, give it a social motive, something to tell, and you have a work of art."

Russian psychologist Lev Vygotsky theorized that we learn first through person-to-person interactions and then individually internalize knowledge until we arrive at deep understanding. Unlike Piaget, who compares development to a ladder, Vygotsky sees development as a spiral, the mechanism he envisions for internalizing knowledge after first experiencing it with an adult mentor. The interactive classroom puts into practice the belief in the social process of idea making. Vygotsky promoted skillful questioning by teachers to guide social interactions in the classroom. No matter what the activity—creating a collage, setting up a pantomime, or developing photographs—it can be interactive.

## Dynamic Intelligence

Israeli educator Reuven Feuerstein worked with traumatized children of the Holocaust. He believed that intelligence is capable of changing and growing and that the teacher needs to guide the discovery process of learning. With stimulation and a rich learning environment, a child's intelligence can undergo some degree of change and can even alter, to some degree, the child's pattern of strengths and weaknesses.

Dr. Jerome Bruner, who also has explored the nature of intellectual growth, believes that a child can learn almost anything if it is presented in a highly organized, simple fashion. This means that the adult has to understand thoroughly the information that he or she is presenting to the student and must be attuned to the child's capacity to absorb the material and to the degree and amount of verbalization the child can understand. Bruner believes that people can teach anything that they thoroughly understand themselves. A good way to communicate a concept to young children is through an art form or some other form of concrete learning.

Harvard psychologist and educator Howard Gardner, who is known for his theory of multiple intelligences, demonstrates that the arts can serve as "entry points," engaging curiosity and improving students' ability to learn because they draw on a whole range of intelligences and learning styles. Gardner's work promotes the integration of the arts in all classrooms.

Marian Diamond, a current pioneering California neurobiologist, describes the growth of dendrites in the brain as the development of "magic trees of the mind." Diamond's research proves that the sights and sounds of enriched school environments cause dendrites to form neural pathways of insight. The brain's interconnected neurons sprout and branch when given the appropriate sensory, mental, and physical stimulation. Her data demonstrate that the curious mind, stimulated to further inquiry, makes the cerebral cortex thicker and the brain more developed. Hands-on activities, experiential learning, and arts-based teaching fit this model.

## Total Involvement

Involvement is the key to success for exceptional learners. Children who cannot read often cannot absorb information well through listening and have trouble organizing the material they do learn. Usually they struggle to convey verbally or in writing what they understand. However, these children do have their own unique ways to take in information and express it. Teachers have to involve their students in learning through the use of many different intelligences. Touching silk or seeing silkworms at work helps some students commit to memory one of China's great products. Walking on a map that has been drawn on a classroom floor helps another child to see the location of Maryland in relation to Delaware and Pennsylvania. Most children—regardless of whether they need them as primary memory tools—enjoy these activities.

To fully appreciate the value of experiential education to exceptional learners, it is important to understand how information is acquired, organized, and remembered. The information we acquire is linked to our experiences. Each new experience is compared with past experiences, sorted, categorized, and then filed in a compartment of the brain; each new experience is much like a library book that is organized on a particular shelf or a document that is stored in computer folders for future retrieval.

The process of sorting and classifying is begun in infancy when we begin to take in the world around us using our bodies as a point of reference. As preschoolers, we begin to have experiences with our environment through play. Play is the beginning of education. It is through play that children begin to develop an information base. They begin to organize the world around them, making connections and discovering relationships. They learn to separate tall from short, round from square, blue from red. Through play, a preschooler learns to compare, find similarities, and generalize. These discoveries then are classified and sorted into categories. This process is vital to the successful storage and retrieval of information at school.

## The Relevance of Preschool Skills

It is my firm belief that many children with learning disabilities have not acquired skills that children typically learn during the preschool years; however, while teaching these skills—basic differentiation of textures, colors, shapes, and sizes—the educator must respect the child's chronological age and use age-appropriate vocabulary and materials. Preschool learning is all about sorting objects, pictures, sounds, animals, people, and toys and observing similarities and differences among these things. This information all gets classified into a mental filing system so that, for example, when a teacher uses the words "tall" and "short," the child's mind retrieves pictures of tall and short people, tall and short animals, tall and short objects at home, and tall and short buildings. If the filing system is in good order, it will work successfully in a first-grade classroom. If the information is diffuse, the child will not be able to retrieve information at will in first grade. Connections will not be made, and relationships will not make sense.

Studying Aesop's fables in drama, making the costumes, setting the scenes, and acting out the fables help children to sort out differences and similarities in human characteristics and to determine the moral of a story. Critical thinking is used to evaluate whether the moral of the story is appropriate. Connections and relationships are made. All of these activities contribute to building necessary academic attributes: memory, comparisons, analysis, and synthesis.

## Information Recall

Recently, a great deal of attention has been focused on the process of storing and retrieving information. A number of educational theorists believe that children with learning disabilities may lack the ability to store information in meaningful components called *schemas* and, therefore, are unable to recall information in an efficient manner. Schemas are organized structures of knowledge that assist us in understanding and recalling events and information. Early work in *schema theory* can be traced to F.C. Bartlett, who claimed [in the 1932 book *Remembering*] that memory is not just rote recall but is reconstructive. The new information we obtain interacts with our prior knowledge, allowing us to reconstruct and construe new meanings. New schemata are created while old ones are reactivated. Subscribers to current schema theory encourage active involvement on the part of the learner along with the teacher; this strategy makes the child with learning disabilities aware of shemata and of the context and interrelationships associated with them. Schema theory explains why concrete approaches in the classroom can help trigger memory. For example, some children best remember the pythagorean theory in algebra by constructing a kite using the theory.

When there is no schema, there is no "hook" on which to hang new information; therefore, the information cannot be remembered. In order to develop appropriate schemas to facilitate conceptual understanding, teachers need to provide exceptional learners with a structure that activates previous experiences. Children remember experiences that touch their lives and give them pleasure. Often, the public becomes afraid when children appear to be playing or having too much fun at school, but it is possible to have fun while participating in well-planned academic activities that are highly intellectual.

> Thirteen 6- and 7-year-olds were pretending to be in a space station. The commander and her 12-person crew were exploring the vast unknown of outer space when a real event occurred. Shoemaker Levy 9, an asteroid that had fallen out of its orbit, was heading straight for Jupiter. Aboard the space station, the crew was alarmed at the possible ramifications of the event. Therefore, the commander and the crew did a detailed analysis of the events.

> The Shoemaker Levy 9 had divided into six fragments, which were all given an alphabetical code (A,B,C,D,E,F). Each of the children represented a piece of the Shoemaker Levy 9. An enormous yellow ball represented Jupiter. The children lined up and intermittently spun and collided into the yellow ball. Upon contact with Jupiter the children would place a black paper on it. The black paper represented a nuclear reaction that took place (each nuclear reaction caused a "bruise-like" effect on the surface of Jupiter). In order to help the children remember the name Shoemaker Levy 9, the children pointed at their shoes and then made the form of a hammer and pointed it at the shoe. For "Le" the children made an "L" with their hand; for "VY," the children made a "V" with their hands; and for "9" they held up nine fingers. With this kinesthetic reinforcement they rarely, if ever, forgot the word. They enjoyed gesturing the name Shoemaker Levy 9, and they remembered a historic event with the correct name that most people have never learned or, hence, have forgotten. Experiences like this can lead to further exploration of the planets, the galaxies, or cosmic events.

## Developing Critical Thinking

Exceptional learners need to be provided with enough opportunities to evaluate whether something is working and to anticipate problems and predict outcomes. They also must learn concrete strategies for approaching tasks, acquiring information, and solving problems. They likely will need help in developing strategies for learning new material, remembering names, memorizing directions, and attending to tasks. They must be encouraged to formulate questions despite conceptual and linguistic difficulties. The arts include a large variety of activities, and learning to ask appropriate questions is part of the plan. "What do we ask?" is a favorite question that teachers use to jolt students into seeking knowledge. A commitment to inquiry leads to a lifetime of learning.

The Lab School approach uses projects, life experiences, concrete materials, and all of the art forms to create active learning to enhance sensory motor development and promote personal, academic, and intellectual development. The acquisition of preschool skills lays the foundation for solid academic learning and intellectual pursuits. Learning to discriminate one thing from another and to integrate several things at once is part of the preschool agenda. The arts provide preschool experiences in a creative way that respects the chronological ages of the children. Students who cannot read, are poor readers, or have learning disabilities and/or ADHD learn well through concrete visual activities that use the senses and multiple intelligences.

# THE HARMFUL EFFECTS OF LABELING STUDENTS

Mel Levine, interviewed by Carin Gorrell

Pediatrician Mel Levine is the director of the Clinical Center for the Study of Development and Learning at the University of North Carolina in Chapel Hill. He is also the founder of All Kinds of Minds, an organization that advocates an optimistic approach toward helping children with learning difficulties. In the following selection, Levine describes his program's philosophy in an interview with Carin Gorrell, senior editor of *Psychology Today*. In Levine's view, the educational system needs to stop the negative process of labeling children as having certain learning disabilities. These labels encourage educators to focus only on a child's problems, he argues. Instead, Levine believes that each child's unique strengths and weaknesses should be evaluated in a holistic manner, with the goal of developing an individualized learning plan based on the child's aptitudes and capabilities.

Mel Levine, M.D., doesn't believe in a one-size-fits-all education. Instead, the Harvard-educated physician and education expert is challenging parents and teachers to develop individual management plans that are unique to each child's personal struggles. A pediatrics professor at the University of North Carolina at Chapel Hill and director of the university's Clinical Center for the Study of Development and Learning, Levine is also founder of All Kinds of Minds. This not-for-profit organization studies eight neurodevelopmental constructs that affect learning—attention, language, memory, neuromotor function, spacial ordering, temporal-sequential ordering, higher-order cognition and social cognition. Using the program's findings, Levine is working to nix negative labels and help educators and families overcome children's learning, developmental and behavioral hurdles with a more optimistic approach. Here, he speaks with *Psychology Today* Senior Editor Carin Gorrell about his brain-based methodology.

*Carin Gorrell: What do you think about the term "learning styles"?*

Mel Levine: It has gotten contaminated. The "learning-styles program" became a kind of cult. It was run irresponsibly and for commercial gain: Its advocates charged schools thousands of dollars to teach about left brain versus right brain. But asking which side of your brain you think with is an oversimplification. For that reason we never use this term. I use "learning differences."

*How did you develop the eight constructs?*

Through seeing patients, clinical experience, keeping pace with the literature and recognizing that people who treat kids with learning difficulties tend to have fairly narrow views. Somebody who diagnoses attention deficits may label too many kids "ADD"; people who study language diagnose most problems as language disorders; neuropsychologists identify everything as a nonverbal learning disability. Everybody has a back-pocket diagnosis. In my opinion, everybody has only a piece of the truth. They neglect to consider how kids are wired—how language affects attention or how memory impacts language and attention. We needed to develop a model that has more of a profiling orientation than a labeling one. To make a profile we had to decide on the major ingredients, so we came up with the eight constructs. Within each construct, of course, there are more specific functions—types of memory, components of language—and one can get as detailed as one wants. The basic philosophy underlying this was "Let's stop reducing children by using labels like ADD or LD."

*Do you believe these disorders exist?*

I don't even like to think they exist. I believe there are some children who have trouble with attention, but labeling all of them ADD doesn't make sense to me. It implies some homogeneity that doesn't exist. Labels oversimplify kids—they don't take into account a child's strengths. Labels are pessimistic because they imply you're always going to be one way.

## Focusing on Optimism and Strengths

*Your program focuses a lot on optimism.*

Optimism, strengths, possibilities—we're trying to use a much less pathological view. We substitute description for labeling—rich description with much greater specificity about where the breakdown is occurring. When a child has trouble with writing, instead of calling it dysgraphia we ask, "Is it a motor problem? A language problem? An organization problem? Trouble generating ideas?" And so on.

*How do you find the answers?*

By looking at samples of the kid's work, getting the observations of his teachers and parents, asking the kid—that's very important. "Why do *you* think you're having trouble writing?" How he responds can provide valuable information: "Because my hand hurts" or "I have some terrific ideas, but I can never figure out how to say them." Routinely, people never bother to ask the kid to be a part of the diagnostic team. We also do direct testing of certain functions—motor function, expressive language, aspects of memory. The goal is not to generate a bunch of test scores. In a funny way, it's like a medical model. When I do a physical exam, I don't score it. I'm doing the same thing when I evaluate a child—I want to know where the weaknesses and strengths are.

*And you show teachers how to respond to these weaknesses?*

And how to make good observations in the classroom. There are a lot of things that are not on a psychology test and yet are very important for success. But if you train teachers to look for them, they will see them every day. So teachers attend our program to learn about each of the constructs, how to observe them at particular ages, how to communicate them and how to demystify the kids. A lot of what we advocate involves helping the kid understand himself. It's based on the premise that you can't work on something if you don't even know what it's called. It's a lot healthier to say, "I'm really smart, but I have a sequencing problem, so I'd better write this stuff down" than to say, "Boy, am I a dummy." And it's remarkable what kids come up with themselves once they have a very clear understanding of what they need to do. That's much more helpful than telling a kid he has ADD.

*How do teachers provide students with this understanding?*

We teach them how to give kids the words and definitions for the problems they need to be working on in a very nonaccusatory, non-sermonizing, amoral kind of way. Everybody has some things they need to be working on.

*Hearing that must be a relief to these children.*

Everybody's got a flawed brain. Some people may not have trouble until they're 30, but others may have troubles kicking in around fifth grade.

*Can these constructs be applied to adult learning?*

Absolutely. These issues are present throughout life.

*So this could help college and continuing-education students.*

And it could impact career choices. I'm always fascinated by people who pick a career that they're very interested in but not wired for.

*How can adults better understand their own learning profile?*

First, do some introspection. Second, there are clinicians who test adults concerned about their own strengths and weaknesses. And by the way, I think grown-ups and parents have to become much wiser consumers of evaluations. They need to ask good questions, rather than simply saying, "I'm having my kid tested."

## The Pros and Cons of Home Schooling

*Are there kids who learn better in a home setting?*

There are a lot of reasons for home schooling: If school personnel have no sensitivity toward your child's struggles—if they keep saying he's immature or not too bright—they've written him off and you've done all you can. Another reason is when a kid is being brutalized by his peers, he may need time out of the jungle to recuperate. From the moment a child gets up in the morning until he's tucked in at night, there's one central mission: avoid humiliation at all costs. If you feel your kid is being humiliated repeatedly in school, you have to do something. Kids have very little insulation.

*Ideally, though, you suggest getting them back into school. What are they missing while at home?*

Most of all, they're missing the social and political experience of school, though probably not much else. Sometimes home schooling engenders tension between the parent and the child because some parents find it hard to assume two roles, but others pull it off quite well.

*Do parents go through your program?*

No, but I'm hoping they'll read my book, *A Mind at a Time*. One purpose of the book is to educate parents so they can be tougher consumers of their kids' education and testing, as opposed to just having blind faith. It's hard to advocate for your kid if you don't know what you're talking about. Parents who have a kid who's struggling in school need to become very knowledgeable about how learning works, where it's breaking down in their child and what the words to describe it are.

# CHAPTER 4

# PEOPLE WITH LEARNING DISABILITIES: PERSONAL NARRATIVES

# My Journey Through the World of Special Education

Christopher Lee and Rosemary Jackson

Christopher Lee is the founder of Disability Resource Associates in Atlanta, Georgia, which provides training and services to individuals with learning disabilities. Along with his coauthor, Rosemary Jackson, a special education professor at Georgia College and State University in Milledgeville, Lee has written two books: *Faking It: A Look into the Mind of a Creative Learner*, and *What About Me? Strategies for Teaching Misunderstood Learners*, from which the following selection is taken. Lee explains that he was diagnosed with dyslexia in the second grade and subsequently was sent through a slew of special education programs. Most of these programs did not meet his particular needs, he recalls; instead, he simply felt stigmatized as stupid and slow. Lee describes his long struggle in the public education system and how he finally began to rebuild his damaged self-esteem through success in sports.

Jacob is not quite a year old. With blond hair, blue eyes, he mimics me as I make faces above him. Stretching and wiggling around the crib, Jacob can barely control himself as his active little body responds to the new stimulus leaning over his crib. Taking in this miracle baby, I find myself without breath and pondering whether or not Jacob will grow up with the same struggles and difficulties as his father and I. I ask myself the same question every time I see him: Does Jacob have a learning disability? Will the genetic strand continue to disrupt the next generation, my nephew, Jacob? . . .

Thirty-five percent of students identified as having learning disabilities drop out of high school, contributing greatly to the nation's drop-out rates. Learning disabilities and substance abuse are the most common impediments to keeping welfare recipients from becoming and remaining employed, according to a 1992 report from the Office of the Inspector General. It is estimated that between 50 and 80 percent of students in Adult Basic Education classes have learning disabilities. The number of prison inmates with learning disabilities ranges from 30 to 50 percent. In order for Jacob not to fall into this pool of negative statistics, it will take several key components merging together at points throughout his life to ensure smooth transitions and positive outcomes.

Life is made up of a continuance of short-term and long-term goals. The very first, raw, primal goal is established at birth, usually by the parents. They want to ensure—no matter what it takes—that this child will have a happy and fulfilling life.

Baby Jacob has all the love in the world and will hopefully grow up to reach this goal. If Jacob had been born with some type of physical disability, this goal would be tougher to reach. Specific and crucial components would need to be put into place in order for Jacob to fulfill his parents' basic goal. A physical disability is usually obvious from the beginning. The parents automatically begin to readjust their expectations and often become frightened about what the future will hold for their child. If Jacob has been born with a learning disability, several years might pass before his parents begin to realize that Baby Jacob is not meeting their or society's expectations. Dreams will diminish day by day as parents and teachers become complacent with the idea that Baby Jacob will fall short of the primal goal.

## A Change in Goals

After I was valuated and *found out* (that I had a learning disability) in the second grade, my parents started to readjust their original goal for my life. I am sure that they still believed I would obtain a fulfilling life even though they now had to deal with this "glitch," a temporary problem focused around my academic achievement. I can imagine my dad saying, "Everything will be fine," denial setting in. "Christopher will just have to work harder. If we stay on the teachers' backs, things will work out." My mother, being the patient and practical one in the family, knew something was deeply wrong. She not only realized that I was dealing with difficulties forming letters and reading words, but also sensed that an emotional struggle was beginning to brew deep within her child. As a second grader I remember feeling an emotional conflict within myself. I was different from the other children around me. Thoughts and words did not come easy for me. Language became my adversary. I failed the second grade. . . .

It was at this point that my parents' long-term goal—my achieving a happy and fulfilling life—began to be replaced by a series of short-term goals: read this word, pass this test, complete this page of math problems—get out of the second grade so you can start all of this over in the third grade. Every bit of effort and energy on the part of my parents, teachers, and myself was put into small achievable goals that focused on basic remediation. At no time do I ever remember anyone telling me that by learning to read and write, one day I could become President of the United States—or, better yet, the New Millennium version of success: President of Microsoft, Inc. Instead, I began a long journey through the world of special education. . . .

## A Frightening Journey

My struggles started in the first grade. I was a failure by the second. Pulled out, I was placed in a separate school, my county's answer to dealing with its population of students with special needs. My journey through special education had begun. I rode a special bus—a smaller bus designed to carry students who use wheelchairs, students who are deaf and blind, and students who look very different from most people, all heading to the same place.

I remember feeling scared and lost. How could my parents take me away from my friends and put me in this place . . . a place that I felt I didn't belong? Unlike the other students on this bus, I could walk and talk and see and hear. As I think back to that time, I'm sure there were other students with labels like mine, but they faded into the background, while the people with physical disabilities were magnified. For the first few months, I felt pity for them. I must have believed I was better than they were because I had capabilities they didn't. From the outside I looked normal and they didn't. Katie always sat in the back of the bus with the other children who used wheelchairs. At first glance, Katie frightened me. She looked so different from the girls I had ridden with the year before. She had light brown hair that was always matted because of the headrest on the wheelchair. She had some movement in her arms, but it was jerky and took much effort. Her speech was slurred at times and missing words, like holes in Swiss cheese. Alice always sat right behind the driver, facing forward, as if she controlled the bus. Throughout our journey to school, Alice would turn her head to look behind at the rest of us. She was the caretaker of the bus. She would scold us for being too loud but was ready to help anyone who needed it. She stood much taller than the rest of us and wore thick red glasses, which, she told me later, prevented the sun from reaching her sensitive eyes. Her skin and hair were white and pasty like Elmer's glue. Robert James, always called by both names, was the only African American on the bus. He was skinny and short, about my size, and always sat in the same seat. He wore thick dark glasses and used a silver stick that he scraped along the ground. I learned to listen for the windshield wiper sound he made as he walked. I remember going home some days and trying to copy Robert James, whittling my own canes from sticks in the woods and trying to find my way back to my house. I was fascinated with Robert James and how he managed to go from the lunchroom to the restroom to the playground without missing a beat.

## Another Adjustment

In the beginning, I was a scared kid. During those first few months of stepping onto that school bus, I truly believed I did not belong. I was not like these kids! However, over the course of a year, things changed. Without realizing it, I began to make friends with each one of these "misplaced" kids. Looking back, my most vivid memories of Katie and Alice and Robert James were not of their disabilities, but of their capabilities. Katie had the ability to connect with people through her sparkling eyes. It's hard to describe, but I felt good being around her. Her eyes gave me truth. Alice showed me how to be strong. Robert James spurred my imagination. By the end of the school year, I was no longer scared of my new friends. By watching them, I knew deep down that they were much smarter than I was, even with their obvious disabilities. I was beginning to figure out why I was a passenger on the little yellow school bus.

The next September rolled around too soon, and before I knew it I was beginning second grade all over in a brand new school. I clearly remember that first day of school. The desk was cold and hard as I slipped quietly into it. The desk was nothing like the soft sand and warm water I played in all summer. This was not a beach, and I was not looking forward to repeating the second grade at this brand new school. Even though I was a year older than the other students around me, I did not feel bigger or smarter. The large room was filled with strangers. My friends were at another school. My eyes kept drifting toward the window in the far corner of the room. It was a small window, but just large enough for me to crawl through, which is exactly what I wanted to do. I quickly noticed that my parents had decided to put me back in with kids that looked like me. No longer were there kids like Katie, Alice, or Robert James. Instead of being in a whole school of kids who didn't fit in, now those of us who were different were simply moved throughout the day to the "Stupid Trailers" behind the school. In these "resource rooms," there were "special" teachers who were supposed to fix my brain with "magical" books, cards, and games. For the next several years, I found myself continuously being pulled out of my regular classes to go not only to the Stupid Trailer, but also to the speech class down the hall. It didn't seem to matter where I went or what class I was in, words and letters and numbers would not stand still or hold their shapes long enough for me to grasp them.

## Finding Some Acceptance

Grade after grade went by. I hated school. I hated myself. By the fifth grade, I was an eleven-year-old boy with an extremely low self-concept. I was a boy who could not learn by traditional methods. Education had not met the challenge of teaching me. My mother continued to work with the school system, attending teacher conferences and arranging tutoring sessions. However, my father went a different route, focusing not on the education system, but on sports. For the first time, I had a glimpse of something positive to pull through that classroom window I always wanted to crawl out of. The sport of swimming became my lifeline. I ended my journey through special education at the end of the ninth grade, when my parents and I decided to move forward rather than remain behind in the special education system. This was the first time I was given an active voice in this important decision. In the back of my mind, I hoped that not having to attend those special education classes meant that I was "fixed." I was still a long way from facing my disability head-on.

Accepting that there is no choice in certain aspects of who I am has been the hardest thing I have ever dealt with. Growing up as an athlete, I have always wanted to be taller and stronger. When I was younger, my father put me on a weight-training program that built muscle mass. However, there was no special program that could make me taller. If there were, I would have found it. It frustrates me that I can control one part of my life but not another. I could control how strong I was through discipline and working out every day with weights, molding my body into what I wanted it to look like. However, no matter how many hours I spent hanging upside down suspended from my closet doorway, I never forced my body to meet my 6'2" ideal. I have learned and accepted that my height is a part of who I am and something over which I have no control (until science invents that Tall Pill). I don't have to like it; I do have to accept it. This statement couldn't be more relevant to how I feel about my learning disabilities. Accepting that there is no choice in certain aspects of who I am has been very difficult.

I believe that if I had been involved from the beginning in the decision-making process related to my special education placements, I might have come to terms with my learning disabilities much sooner. I know that my parents and teachers all thought they were doing what was best for me, but I never understood why I had to go to a special school or to the Stupid Trailers, and no one ever asked for my opinion. Fortunately, things are done differently today. Both students and parents are now encouraged to participate in decisions about where in the school system a student with special needs can best be served. Another change for the better is the developing philosophy that students with disabilities can and should be educated with their peers in the regular classroom. Teachers have found over the years that the strategies used by special educators can also be beneficial to use with students who have no learning difficulties. Using these strategies, along with appropriate accommodations for special needs students, teachers can now teach to a diverse range of students. This concept is called *inclusion*. . . .

The concept of inclusion has changed tremendously over the last twenty-five years. In the beginning, with the passage of laws making it illegal to exclude children with disabilities from public education, the concept was called *mainstreaming*. This focused on making sure that all students received the same education as those who had no disabilities and that special education support systems were developed to help these students succeed. I am a product of that time. If the concept of mainstreaming had not come about, it is likely that I would have completed my entire school career in a special school similar to the one I attended in the second grade. As it was, I became a vital part of the transition era; I was a guinea pig for all the experimental methods being tried out during the 1970s.

# When School Troubles Come Home: The Effect on a Family

Curt Dudley-Marling

Curt Dudley-Marling is a professor in the Lynch School of Education at Boston College and coauthor of *Readers and Writers with a Difference: A Holistic Approach to Teaching Literacy to LD and Remedial Students*. In the following excerpt from his book *A Family Affair: When School Troubles Come Home*, Dudley-Marling confesses that his background in the field of education did not prepare him to deal with the learning difficulties that his own daughter, Anne, exhibited from an early age. He explains that he and his wife, two successful and highly educated professionals, were flummoxed by Anne's academic problems, especially since she was obviously a bright child. He and his wife grew increasingly anxious over his daughter's struggles in school, the author relates, and disagreements over the best course of action to take concerning Anne's problems put a strain on their marriage. Furthermore, Dudley-Marling writes, their relationship with their daughter was marred by tension over grades and stressful homework sessions. Only after Anne was accepted into an alternative school did her academic work—and the atmosphere within the family—improve, he concludes.

I am a professor of education at Boston College. I am also an author, researcher, teacher educator, and journal editor whose work focuses mainly on children for whom school learning is sometimes a struggle. I have been a teacher of students with learning disabilities and children who are developmentally delayed. I have taught in a third-grade classroom that included students who struggled academically. In my professional life, I have learned to appreciate the important role parents can play in their children's schooling and I have, in my writing, encouraged other educators to find ways to involve parents in their children's schoolwork. I have, however, also seen the ways schooling can become an unwelcome intrusion in the lives of families, especially for families whose children have been labelled "exceptional.". . .

My interest in the effect of school troubles on the lives of families would seem to be a logical extension of my work with students who struggle in school; however, my primary interest in this topic is personal. Besides being a professional educator, I am also a parent who has experienced firsthand the pain and frustration of having a child who struggles in school. As a parent, I have learned that even relatively minor problems in school can have far-reaching consequences for family life. . . .

Of course, how my wife and I experienced our daughter's schooling is part of the larger story of our life as a family and our hopes and aspirations for our children. It is within this broader context of our hopes and aspirations for our daughter, Anne, that I begin by sharing *our* story. The following excerpt from a journal my wife and I kept for Anne during the first eighteen months of her life provides a good starting point for talking about the effects of school trouble on my family.

## Anne's Birth: Expecting the Best

Dear Anne,

We've decided to keep a journal for you. This rather long first entry is about yesterday, September 28, 1982, the day you were born.

Chris's labor was long and difficult. We arrived at the hospital Monday evening and, by Tuesday afternoon, Chris and I were tired and discouraged. Then, early Tuesday evening, we were told that you—our first child—might be in distress, but we'd have to "wait and see." In the meantime, we had to endure a fetal heart monitor, which was strapped to your mother's abdomen. This machine produced a continuous readout of your heartbeat, which gave us plenty to worry about. By 8:00 it was apparent you were in serious trouble and the doctor ordered Chris moved to the delivery room "double quick," as she put it. Since you were "already in the birth canal," the doctor used forceps to pull you out. And, boy, did she ever pull. With one foot braced against the operating table for leverage, she nearly pulled Chris off the table. It didn't take long before we learned what the problem was. The umbilical cord was wrapped around your neck twice. The doctor quickly cut the cord and turned you over to an intensive care nurse who had been standing by. The nurse suctioned your mouth, gave you oxygen, and cleaned you up. The medical staff told us you had been without oxygen for some undetermined length of time and had been in danger of your life. But, within a few minutes, all your vital signs looked good and we breathed a sigh of relief.

Still, having feared the worst, Chris and I were in a state of shock. It must have been 5–10 minutes before either of us even thought to ask the predictable, "Is it a girl or a boy?" Within a very short time I carried you down to intensive care—you in one arm, and an oxygen tube that I held under your nose, in the other—where you spent the night. I've never been so frightened in my life. Then, while I was in the intensive care nursery, I was given a message to rush to the recovery room because Chris was in trouble. It turned out that she had hemorrhaged and lost two units of blood, but her condition had stabilized by the time I arrived. Exhausted, I left Chris in the recovery room around 10:30. I cried all the way home. I called my dad to give him the news, but I couldn't stop crying. Eventually, I had a couple of glasses of wine and cried myself to sleep. While I was sleeping a nurse brought you to Chris to breast-feed. We're hopeful. . . .

—(Anne's journal, September 29, 1982)

This isn't how I imagined the birth of Anne, our first child. Like most parents, I expected that Chris would be awakened in the middle of the night by *mild* contractions (we knew that babies *always* came around 3:00 in the morning), we'd get dressed, grab the suitcase we'd already packed, and drive to the hospital where, several hours later, Chris would give birth to our daughter or son (we were pretty sure it was going to be a son). Enlightened by our childbirth classes, we took it for granted that we would avoid the sterile, technologically intrusive experience our mothers had when they gave birth to us. We were confident that the birth of our first child would be an intensely spiritual event unencumbered by the technology of childbirth. And, unlike mothers and fathers from our parents' generation, we would experience the transformation from husband and wife to mother and father together.

We did experience Anne's birth together (when my wife read this part she reminded me that, although the nurses frequently expressed their concern that I eat to keep up *my* strength, the pain was all *hers*), but, as my entry in Anne's journal makes clear, nothing else unfolded as we had imagined. And it wasn't that we weren't prepared for the possibility that things could go wrong. We were well aware just how wrong things could go at birth. Up to the time Anne was born, Chris and I had spent the bulk of our professional careers teaching students with developmental disabilities and, for many of these students, mental and physical disabilities could be traced to birth trauma. Additionally, Debbie, the woman who taught our childbirth classes, routinely reminded expectant parents that even *normal* births were often complicated. We *knew* what could happen. We were, however, just as sure these things happened only to other people.

## The First Trying Time

We were also aware that Anne's traumatic birth put her at risk for a range of disabilities, so we actively searched for evidence that Anne was OK and we were easily alarmed by any sign of a problem. I will never forget the day—exactly one week after Anne's birth—when Marilyn, one of the secretaries in my department at the University of Colorado, interrupted an undergraduate class I was teaching to tell me that Chris was trying to reach me because "there seemed to be something wrong with Anne." Marilyn insisted that I dismiss my class and call my wife "immediately," which I did.

Chris, who had extensive training in the treatment of children with cerebral palsy, had been unable to elicit a particular reflex in Anne which she took as a possible indication of cerebral palsy. In less than an hour I met my wife at the office of Larry Waldman, our daughter's pediatrician. Dr. Waldman also observed in Anne either an unwillingness or an inability to use her right arm. He agreed that this could indicate a neurological problem, although it was, as he was quick to point out, "too early" to diagnose cerebral palsy. "We will just have to wait and see," he told us. Dr. Waldman also ordered an X ray of Anne's collarbone on the chance that the routine check for a broken collarbone at the hospital had missed something. Every parent knows how long the thirty minutes we waited for the results of the X ray lasted. It's also easy to imagine our joy—and relief—when Dr. Waldman caught our eye as he walked toward the waiting area and communicated the results of the X ray to us by pantomiming the breaking of a stick. As I'm writing this chapter, I have lived on this earth for more than fifty years and two of the most emotional moments in my life occurred within the space of a week.

Once again, we felt that we had dodged the proverbial bullet. We no longer feared the worst and, as Anne developed, even our smallest worries evaporated. Before the end of her tenth month Anne took her first steps and uttered her first word ("doggie," not "daddy" as I might have hoped). She had just turned two when she told me, "I have a lot of important work to do" as she helped with the housework. On that September morning in 1988, when we waited at the corner for the yellow school bus that would carry Anne—our clever, sociable, and highly verbal daughter—to the school where she would begin first grade, we had few doubts that everything was going to be fine.

## First Grade: Signs of Trouble

Anne boarded the school bus happily each morning and every night she'd spend literally hours telling us all about school, especially her new friend, Lisa, who had just moved to Toronto from South Africa. Anne was happy and so were we. After all, school trouble only happened to other people's children.

The first sign that all was not well came in late November during a parent-teacher conference with Anne's first-grade teacher. As her teacher put it, Anne was "happy, likeable, but *young*." Anne's teacher didn't specify any particular problems, but the way she intoned the word *young* troubled us for days. In our professional lives we had often heard teachers use *young* as a euphemism for *immature, delayed,* or even *slow*. We began to pay much closer attention to what was happening at school and my wife, Chris, was nearly consumed by her worries about Anne.

In March 1989, Anne's report card stated that "Anne is making *slow* but steady progress in the first grade program . . . and completes work *to the best of her ability*." We were immediately afflicted with a kind of tunnel vision that blurred everything on the page except the words *slow but steady* and *to the best of her ability*. The end-of-year report card from the first-grade teacher reiterated that "Anne [had] worked hard and made slow but steady progress" and "It will be necessary for her to complete expectations in the Grade 1 program before beginning work at the Grade 2 level." In other words, Anne had not completed the expectations for first grade. After reading Anne's end-of-year report, Chris was so distraught over "Anne's future" that she didn't sleep for days. "Anne can't read," she said. "They're going to put her in special education." "We should have kept her in kindergarten another year." "What's going to happen to Anne when she grows up?" "It's your fault." "It's the fault of the doctor who delivered Anne." "It's my fault." For my part, I played the role of the optimistic father who wanted everything to be fine. "She'll be fine." "Anne just needs more time to develop." "Next year will be a good year." This pattern would repeat itself every time Anne received a report card for the next seven years.

## Continuing Problems

We had imagined that Anne's birth would be spiritually rich and medically uneventful. Clearly, that wasn't how it worked out. We were also confident that Anne would do well in school despite our professional experience (Chris as a speech pathologist and me as a special education teacher), which indicated that many children do not do well in school. But those were *other* people's children. Chris and I had both done well in school and we took it for granted that our clever, sociable, and verbal daughter would also do well in school. We could not even imagine how it could be otherwise. But, whatever we imagined, Anne's school troubles continued as the following excerpt from Anne's first-term report card in second grade indicates.

> Anne is beginning to have more success using phonics skills to decode unfamiliar words. She often has difficulty understanding written directions in her daily work. She must read directions slowly and thoroughly and then think carefully about what she has read. Reading at home will continue to build her vocabulary and improve her fluency in oral reading.

> She needs assistance in selecting material appropriate for her level. Anne's sight vocabulary is slowly developing which is aiding the fluency of her oral reading. She is beginning to copy written language to convey meaning. She enjoys dictating thoughts and ideas to develop a story and uses illustrations to further express her ideas.

Taken at face value, Anne's second-grade teacher's assessment of her reading and writing development sounds promising—she was, after all, "beginning to have more success." We suspected, however, that Anne's teacher was writing in a code meant to comfort parents *and* to alert future teachers to Anne's *problems*. Generally, this code is known only to teachers, but, based on our own observations of Anne's reading and writing, conversations with the teacher, and years of experience working in the schools, we read the teacher's comments to mean:

- Anne is able to sound out a few words and recognize some words on sight, but is generally unsuccessful reading continuous texts.
- You (Anne's parents) are going to have great difficulty finding *any* books Anne will be able to read independently.
- Anne cannot write continuous texts (she copies text and draws pictures).
- You (Anne's parents) need to do more reading with your daughter.
- Anne may not be very bright. ("She must read directions *slowly* and thoroughly and then *think carefully* about what she has read.")

## An Active Role

It may be that we read too much into the teacher's comments, but, nonetheless, this *is* how we felt when we read (and, in Chris's case, reread and reread) Anne's report card. For the rest of the school year, we debated and quarrelled over the meaning of Anne's report cards and how we should respond. Was Anne merely immature or was she less able than her classmates? Did she have a learning disability? Should we have her tested? Would everything be OK as her first grade teacher suggested? Who was to blame? What should *we* do?

Although we generally disagreed on how to respond to Anne's struggles in school, we did agree that we needed to take a more active role in teaching Anne to read. Up to this point we had read to Anne (at least) every night, provided her with an extensive collection of quality children's literature, and demonstrated our own interest in print (our house is full of books and we read all the time). We had not, however, made any sort of systematic effort to *teach* Anne to read. This all changed with her first-term report card in second grade. We began by increasing significantly the amount of time we read to Anne each day. We also made more of an effort to draw Anne's attention to the print on the page by (sometimes) pointing to words in the text as we read. When the text was particularly predictable—and we made a conscious effort to read predictable books with Anne—we often pointed to a word and asked Anne to tell us what the word was. We sometimes asked Anne to read along with us, in which case we'd lower our voices when Anne was able to take control of the text and raise our voices when she stumbled, a technique called *assisted reading.* To make it easier for Anne to read along with us, we often read the same book with her many times over a period of several days, a technique called *repeated reading.* Finally, we told Anne she could keep her bedroom light on for an extra thirty minutes after bedtime *if* she spent the time looking at books. (I'm pretty sure that this turned out to be the most powerful factor in getting Anne to engage with texts.)

## The Burden of Homework

By the time Anne started third grade she was reading at least at grade level and, within a couple of years, she was a better than average reader. Despite her improvement as a reader, Anne's school troubles only got worse. Third grade seemed to go better for Anne, but her final report card contained the ominous warning that "Anne still has some problems that should be addressed." By fourth grade it was painfully apparent what these "problems" were. Anne had become a good reader whose "comprehension of material read [was] very good" and her "written efforts [were] growing in sophistication." However, according to her teacher, she had great difficulty organizing her work and, as a result, Anne often failed to complete her work at school. When she did complete her work it was often misplaced or lost so schoolwork often had to be completed (or redone) at home. And it was uncompleted work at school in the form of homework that had a particularly disruptive effect on our family life. Since Anne often didn't finish her work at school, she tended to have *more* homework than her peers. Because she was less organized than most of her peers, it also took her *longer* to complete her homework.

Homework was generally an unwelcome intrusion in our lives. Homework affected my relationship with my wife, my son, and, of course, Anne. Some nights Anne began her homework right after dinner and worked on schoolwork past her normal bedtime. When this wasn't enough time to complete her assignments, we'd wake Anne at 6:00 the next morning to complete her homework. Some evenings we'd end up embarrassing Anne by taking her back to school to retrieve work she'd forgotten to bring home. Homework sessions usually began with gentle encouragement, but the anger and resentment we felt—at the teachers for assigning so much homework and at Anne for her seeming indifference to the demands of her teachers—often bubbled over and we'd find ourselves yelling at Anne and each other. The explosion of emotion that resulted from the discovery that Anne had lost eight weeks' worth of work on her "major project" in fourth grade was not a proud moment in my parenting career. Nor can I even remember what our son (four years younger than Anne) usually did while we *helped* Anne with her homework, but he wasn't getting much attention from us. (I cringe to think what Anne and Ian learned about parenting from these interactions.) Homework gave us little time to ride our bikes, walk in the woods, fly our kite, or play fetch with our dog at the park. It is no wonder that some nights I readily accepted Anne's assurances that she had no homework or *forgot* even to ask if she had any.

When Anne was in fourth grade, a student in one of my undergraduate classes asserted that homework was a good way to encourage parents to spend more time with their children. No doubt some teachers feel this way. Yes, homework did encourage (more like *require*) Chris and I to spend more time with Anne, but it was not time anyone in our family remembers fondly. Homework was merely a way for the unpleasantness Anne experienced in school to spill over into our family life. It is probably for this reason that I learned to hate homework. When Anne was in elementary school I came to deeply resent homework as an intrusion into our family life and I didn't have good feelings about the teachers who thought they were doing us or Anne a favor by assigning it.

## Marital Stress

A friend of mine once suggested that living with another person was one of the hardest things most of us tried to do. I agree. Negotiating a life with another person is one of the most joyous aspects of our lives but, even under the best of circumstances, maintaining a long-term relationship with another adult isn't easy. The presence of children often adds to the challenge of maintaining a happy, healthy marital relationship as couples are forced to renegotiate their relationships to account for the presence of new family members. It may be doubly difficult to maintain a healthy marriage when *school troubles* become a focus of family relationships. This was certainly true in our house where the constant tension around Anne's schooling sometimes took its toll on our marriage. Since we tried not to yell at Anne—and we couldn't yell at the teacher although there were a few nasty notes—we occasionally took our frustrations out on each other.

Chris and I were rarely able to agree on how to respond to Anne's school troubles. I wanted to be patient and support Anne at home. "Give her some time and she'll be fine," I'd counsel. Chris favored a more interventionist approach: "Let's get Anne tested." "We should demand more from the teacher and the school." "Maybe Anne needs special education." "Do *something*." Out of concern and frustration— and without my knowledge—Chris arranged for Anne to be tested privately during the summer between third and fourth grade by a psychologist with whom she worked. To this day I have never read the psychologist's report although Chris tells me that Anne has "above average intelligence." Nevertheless, this incident was just one more source of tension in our lives.

Another source of contention was Chris's demand that I should have done more to move the school to provide more support for Anne. "Use your influence," she'd say, "Make them do something to help Anne," although it was never clear to me what I might influence the school to do. More to the point, although I was acquainted with the superintendent and the principal, I was loath to ask for any special treatment for Anne. However, when Anne was in fifth grade I finally reached the point where my own anger and frustration—along with the pressure from my wife—overcame my reluctance to "pull a few strings" and I attempted to use my influence with the principal and the superintendent to get Anne some extra help without having her labeled as "exceptional.". . . With the assistance of the principal we elicited several promises from Anne's teacher including, for example, to monitor Anne's work more carefully and to provide Anne with more individual support and direction in the classroom. The special education resource teacher also agreed to work with Anne on an "unofficial" basis which was common practice in this school. As it turned out, the promised support from Anne's regular classroom teacher was never provided although Anne's next report card was the best Anne had ever received (all Bs). Predictably, we grew hopeful. Her final report card, however, was mostly Ds, which made us suspect that the teacher had given Anne higher marks merely to get us off her back. Anne's life at school was not getting better.

The tensions in our household were the worst in the days immediately before and after Anne's report cards came home. My stomach was often a churning mass of worries for several days preceding Anne's report cards as I anticipated the certainty of family turmoil. For Chris, report cards certified that something was wrong with Anne, that we hadn't done enough in support of Anne, and that Anne's future was bleak. "She won't be able to go to college." "She won't even be able to get a good job." For weeks after the receipt of Anne's report cards Chris's anxieties dominated her waking hours and frequently intruded on her sleep. Fatigue brought on by tension and lack of sleep made things look even darker for Chris. I was worried too, but usually I tried to defuse the tension by striking a more optimistic stance (a male problem, I think). "Anne's going to be fine." "We just need to work on her self-confidence." "Lots of people who don't go to college lead happy, fulfilled lives." From Chris's perspective my reassurances indicated only that I wasn't listening to her concerns and the stresses on our relationship worsened. I hoped that we could avoid the stress associated with Anne's schooling by trying not to talk about it since these *discussions* always led to a quarrel. But the regular intrusion of schooling into our lives in the form of homework, report cards, and notes and phone calls from teachers ("Anne didn't hand in . . .") made it impossible for us to ignore Anne's *school troubles*. And the tensions over schooling spilled over into every aspect of my relationships with Chris and Anne.

I don't want to be overly dramatic here by claiming that the tensions that derived from Anne's school troubles drove us to the brink of divorce, although there were moments when this seemed at least a possibility. I can say, however, that, for periods of time, our home was not such a happy place, as school trouble regularly denied us the pleasures of a warm, supportive, and active family life. Recognizing the harm that was being done to our relationship, we finally sought the assistance of a marriage counselor (we were lucky enough to have insurance that paid for marriage counseling) who helped Chris and I to "reopen the lines of communication" between us. I think it was the marriage counselor who finally moved me to intervene directly in Anne's schooling. Our marriage counselor also helped me to acknowledge the stress Chris felt over Anne's struggles in school. . . .

## A Loss of Confidence

From my perspective, the most serious consequence of Anne's struggles in school was the effect on her sense of self. As I was writing this section, I asked Anne to talk to me about how school made her feel when she was at her "old" school. Anne told me that, during those years, she didn't find school interesting. She had no reason to work hard, so she often did poorly. She said that, "I could have done well if wanted to, but I didn't want to." She blamed a particularly poor report card in fifth grade on a letter we had sent to her teacher (and copied to the principal) documenting her teacher's failure to follow through on any of the promises she'd made to us to provide individual support and direction for Anne. The poor end-of-year report was "getting back at me for your letter," Anne said. Anne also recalls a "chain reaction": at her old school, friends were more important to her than school work but, when she did poorly in school, she didn't have any friends, and then she did even more poorly in school. Anne is also quick to blame her school struggles on "awful teachers," "poor explanations of the work," and "unclear expectations."

When I pushed her, Anne finally conceded that her report cards often made her feel stupid. Anne said that she always dreaded report cards and our reaction to them. Homework books (a way of helping us keep track of Anne's school assignments) made her feel especially bad about herself.

> Only the stupid kids had homework books so, if I had a homework book, I must be stupid. . . . Because of the homework books the other kids would make fun of me. "Anne's stupid, She needs a homework book." The homework books made me feel that even my parents thought I was stupid.

Just being reminded of homework books was enough to make Anne mad and she stayed mad at me the rest of the afternoon. In our conversation, Anne also expressed some resentment toward her brother for whom school is "so easy."

My own sense is that Anne's self-esteem was devastated by her school experience. Over the years she began to take almost anything she couldn't do well as evidence that she was "stupid." By seventh grade she was walking around the house with her head down and her shoulders slumped. Making matters worse, her confidence slipped to its lowest point at a time when the social rivalries among the girls in her class were at their height. The worse she felt, the poorer she did in school. The poorer she did in school, the worse Anne felt and the more both she and her classmates constructed her as a victim. It was this vicious cycle that Anne referred to as a "chain reaction." If bringing Anne home from the hospital after her birth is one of my happiest memories, the image of Anne slumping her way to invisibility is one of my saddest.

## The Seventh Grade

Still, even in these *worst of times* there were hopeful signs. In seventh grade, for example, Anne gave a speech in school on the political and historical meaning of fairy tales that was judged the best in her class, winning her the right to participate in a whole-school speech contest to which parents were invited. The same year Anne demonstrated extraordinary determination and stamina when she and I rode our tandem bicycle on a two day, 210-mile tour—most of the ride in the cold, wind, and rain. She was also beginning to read widely for the first time in her life showing a particular preference for Holocaust tales. There was also no doubt that, despite her setbacks at school, Anne was one of the kindest, most caring people we knew.

The end of Anne's year in seventh grade was, however, one of the low points in Anne's life and in our lives as parents. Anne was virtually without friends at school and, worse, some of the girls seemed to derive pleasure from tormenting her. Her end-of-year report card—poor grades and poorer marks for effort—gave us little reason to hope that eighth grade would be any better. On her seventh-grade report card Anne even got a C in French, the one subject in which she had consistently earned As and Bs. The teacher's comments referred to "math and written language skills [that] continue to challenge her [and] Anne is encouraged to review these skills over the summer in preparation for eighth grade." (Our reading: Anne's going to be in *real* trouble in eighth grade.) Our worries about whether or not Anne would attend college were replaced with more immediate worry: How is Anne going to cope with the demands of high school?

At the end of seventh grade we'd had enough. We'd seen plenty of evidence to believe that, under the right circumstances, Anne could do well in school. It was also clear to us, however, that Anne would never thrive in school until she regained the confidence that had seeped slowly away over seven years of schooling until she felt almost worthless. The two-year-old who had "a lot of important work to do" no longer had the confidence even to try. We were even more worried about Anne's taking on the role of victim, a particularly dangerous role for young girls. Something had to change and we pushed Anne hard to consider changing schools, but, early in the summer, Anne refused to even consider the idea. However, by summer's end, after a three week vacation to Great Britain, Anne announced to us that she'd go to school anywhere *but* the school she'd been attending.

## Changing Schools

We encouraged Anne to consider transferring to the Toronto Waldorf School because of the reputation of Waldorf schools for respecting children. Waldorf education, founded in 1919, is an international movement and, because of the emphasis on the "whole child" in Waldorf education, the curriculum gives equal emphasis to music, movement, art, handwork, and traditional academics. As we pondered over the decision to transfer Anne to a Waldorf school, I read that Rudolph Steiner, the founder of Waldorf schools, once said that "Children are God's gift to humanity." This is a central tenet of Waldorf education. If Steiner's aphorism betrays an overly romanticized notion of childhood it also suggests a respect for children as important people and childhood as a significant time of life. And it was respect that Anne was after. When we met with a Waldorf teacher to talk about the school, Anne asked only two questions. First she asked, "Where do the kids at this school eat their lunches?" At Anne's previous school, upper-elementary students ate on the floor of the gym, a practice Anne had found insulting. She also asked the Waldorf teacher, "Do you let your students read the author R.L. Stine?" Since Anne had read little, if any, of R.L. Stine's work, my guess is that she was gauging the Waldorf staff's respect for their students by testing this teacher's willingness to censor her students' reading selections.

In the end, Anne agreed to attend the Toronto Waldorf School even though, because of differences in cutoff dates, it meant a second year in seventh grade. After just one year in a more respectful school environment, Anne began to do better in school. Her confidence soared, she began to develop better work habits, and she was *much* happier. It is not my intention, however, to promote Waldorf education. Creating a respectful learning environment is not unique to Waldorf education. It has been my privilege to have visited many public and private schools across the United States and Canada where respect for children is a basic pedagogical principle. I also doubt that all Waldorf schools fulfill their mission equally well nor do I believe that Waldorf education is the best learning environment for all children. It is just that this alternative has worked well for Anne. Nor do I want to suggest that Anne's school troubles magically disappeared the moment she entered the door of her new school. Missing assignments continued to be a problem in seventh and eighth grade. [At the time of this writing] Anne has just completed her sophomore year at the Waldorf High School in Lexington, Massachusetts, and she continues to do reasonably well in school. We still worry about her work habits sometimes, and because she struggled with trigonometry and logarithms this year we hired a math tutor for the summer. But we're hopeful that her high school experience will be successful and she will be admitted to a *good* college. But our experience over the past sixteen years tells that we shouldn't take anything for granted. High school and college are often difficult times for young people like Anne. The academic demands are going to grow, there will be more homework, and then there's sex, drugs, cars, and alcohol. We know all this from our own experience, but we still can't imagine things won't go well for Anne as she grows into a young woman. Bad things only happen to other people's children.

## Advantages

Clearly, school has not always been a pleasant place for Anne and our experience with Anne's schooling has led to frustration, anger, tension, and, occasionally, despair. Still, I am mindful of the fact that we have been able to deal with Anne's schooling from a position of privilege that has certainly minimized the impact of Anne's academic struggles on her and the rest of her family. Anne had an immediate *advantage* in school because the values and discourse practices of her middle-class home so closely matched the values and discourse practices of the schools. Sharing a common cultural background with Anne's teachers also made it relatively easy for us to communicate with them. Because of our background in education and our own success in school, my wife and I also have a good sense of what schools want from kids. This helped us teach Anne "how to play the game" of schooling (although Anne often rejected this kind of advice). Our professional backgrounds also enabled us to provide substantial instructional support for Anne's reading development when she wasn't learning to read at the rate the school expected. My own professional standing gave me a kind of access to the principal and the superintendent that few parents have although I'm not sure this always helped us with individual teachers. Waldorf education *has* been a factor in reversing Anne's fortunes in school, but this would not have been possible if we didn't have the financial resources to pay expensive private school tuition. As difficult as schooling has been at times for Anne, given a different set of cultural and economic resources the pain of school failure could have been much, much worse.

# An Actor's Method of Coping with Dyslexia

Renee Stovsky

In the following selection, *St. Louis Post-Dispatch* reporter Renee Stovsky profiles Brad Little, a successful stage actor who has dyslexia. Little describes his difficulties in school and remembers being taunted and terrorized by his classmates for being different. He explains that when he was a child, not much was known about dyslexia, and his problem went undiagnosed until he was in high school. Around the same time, Little discovered his musical talents and began excelling in choir and school musicals, which turned his life around. Today, as Stovsky relates, Little continues to hone his craft, appearing on the stage throughout America and Europe. In addition, he takes time out of his busy schedule to connect with students who are struggling with learning disabilities.

Social outcast. It's a role Brad Little plays with relish as the star of *Phantom of the Opera*. It's a role Little would love to have relinquished in real life.

As the masked miscreant lurking in the catacombs of the Paris Opera House in Andrew Lloyd Webber's acclaimed musical, . . . Little unleashes a spectacular reign of terror on stage. But as a boy growing up in Redlands, Calif., Little was terrorized himself by his peers.

"I was beaten up every day after school. . . . I was a loner, or at best a follower. I didn't have many friends," says Little.

## An Invisible Demon

Unlike the phantom, whose hideous facial deformities make him a freak, Little was ostracized because of an invisible demon—dyslexia. The learning disability made it impossible for Little to master the world of the printed word, no matter how hard he tried.

"In the second grade, I couldn't distinguish 'house' from 'horse.' I confused 'th' with 'wh.' I stumbled over any word that had five letters or more. I was a failure when it came to 'Run, Spot, run,'" Little says.

And in those days—Little is in his 30s—neither the teachers at

Mariposa Elementary School in Redlands nor Little's parents knew how to help a child struggling to learn to read.

"No one—not even my father, who was a college professor—could diagnose the problem. By the time I was in sixth grade, I was only reading at a second-grade level, though my math skills were at a 12th-grade level," says Little.

Unfortunately, it wasn't just Little's literary background that suffered. Like many kids living with untreated learning problems, Little's dyslexia led to emotional problems such as low self-esteem.

"I was so frustrated, so angry. Tears would fly down my face during tutoring sessions. I thought I was just stupid," says Little. "I had a neighbor, a boy my age named Mark, who was severely retarded. He drooled. My mother used to tell me that 'Mark was special.' So when I wound up in a special education program myself, I was completely confused. I didn't have Mark's strange behaviors or physical characteristics. I didn't know what was wrong."

And that's why, now that Little is a star—he has appeared in European tours of *Jesus Christ Superstar* and *West Side Story* as well as in Broadway's *Phantom* (he played Raoul), *Cyrano the Musical*, *Fiddler on the Roof* and *Anything Goes*—he makes it a point to take time out from touring to talk to students with learning disabilities.

## Building Bridges to Understanding

In St. Louis, Missouri, where *Phantom* is playing at The Fox Theatre through Sept. 26, 1998, Little spent an afternoon at The Churchill School, a private school in Ladue that serves high-potential kids 8 to 16 years of age with diagnosed learning disabilities. In between regaling his audience with stories of stage calamities, like the time his phantom cape got caught in an elevator, and his friendship with Maya, a cheetah he met at the Cincinnati Zoo, Little imparted a life lesson it took him a long time to learn: You are not alone.

"Do you know what I used to do when we had to read aloud in class?" he confessed to the students. "My teacher would ask each pupil to read one paragraph in a story. I would count the students ahead of me in my row, figure out which paragraph I was going to have to read, and try to memorize it so that when it was my turn, no one would laugh at me. Trouble was, the teacher invariably would tell the girl right in front of me, 'Go on, read another paragraph.' Then I was sunk."

His anecdote hit home; waves of laughter rolled across the school's auditorium.

Little says it wasn't until he landed the role of the phantom that he got the nerve to "come out of the closet" about his dyslexia.

"I suppose I had a natural affinity to the character; I knew what it felt like to be ridiculed," he says. "And my wife (actress Barbara McCulloh) encouraged me to speak out. She told me I had an opportunity to touch somebody out there with the same problem."

So how did Little go from a preteen with terrible self-esteem to a self-assured, highly regarded stage actor? When he was in ninth grade, his father accepting a teaching position overseas and Little's family spent the year in Europe.

"My dad read to me a lot, and I was accepted by the college kids we met. I learned—and I fit in," says Little. "When we returned to southern California, I was scared to death to go back to my own school. So I went to a high school with a program called 'SWAS'—'school within a school'—with a more hands-on approach. They allowed oral instead of written tests there. Within a year, I went from a 1.5 GPA to a 3.6 GPA."

## Finding a Niche

Simple academic success was not Little's only salvation. Finding a label for his problem—his mother realized he had dyslexia after watching a Phil Donahue television segment about it—helped. But discovering and nurturing his musical talent was key. As a high school freshman, he was accepted into the top-echelon choir. He also began landing the lead roles in school musicals.

"I found my niche. And suddenly, to my surprise, I was not only accepted by my peers, I was actually looked up to by them. The word 'special' took on a whole different connotation for me—now I had a 'special talent,'" he says.

Not that his dyslexia was conquered; far from it. Taking the PSATs was "an absolutely terrible" experience, says Little. "I watched everyone around me frantically turning the pages, and I just bawled. I couldn't get through it," he says.

So Little eschewed college aspirations and headed first to Los Angeles, where he worked in local theater, and then New York, where he quickly landed a job in *They're Playing Our Song*.

Nowadays, Little finds ways to compensate for his slow reading. He has a phenomenal memory and relies on tape recordings his wife makes to learn his lines in a script. He also has the uncanny ability to hear something and sing it right back.

"I don't read music—I can't! I listen to the melody and then study the words instead," he says.

Most of all, Little has found self-acceptance. He is finally at peace with who he is—dyslexia and all.

"You know, my wife is a Phi Beta Kappa—book smart. But she's learning disabled when it come to anything logical, like electronics. We all have our quirks—mine just happens to be some kind of page-to-eye-to-brain communication problem," he says.

"When someone asks me how it feels to read backwards now, I'm not ashamed. I just laugh and say, 'How should I know? I don't know what it feels like to read forward!'"

# LEVELING THE PLAYING FIELD FOR STUDENTS WITH LEARNING DISABILITIES

Duane Noriyuki

In the following selection, *Los Angeles Times* writer Duane Noriyuki describes the work of Janeen Steel, a lawyer who runs a program to help low-income families gain access to school services
for children with learning disabilities. As Noriyuki explains, Steel
has a unique qualification for her job: She has personally experienced the pain of feeling lost, stupid, and worthless because of
an undiagnosed learning disability. Frustrated with her academic
difficulties, Steel dropped out of high school and spent many
years jumping from job to job. Finally, after a community college
professor diagnosed her dyslexia, Steel began utilizing services
for students with learning disabilities, which enabled her to
eventually graduate from college and law school. Steel has put
her law degree to use by working to ensure that the Los Angeles
public schools provide appropriate programs and accommodations for students with disabilities, Noriyuki reports.

The art on Janeen Steel's office wall is made of fabric scraps, bits and
pieces painted and placed without pattern or rhythm. She created it
while attending law school. It reflects, she says, a life of fragments,
darkness and chaos, a life reaching for light.

In it, she sees herself as well as others with learning disabilities.

Steel, 39, is director of the Learning Rights Project at the Western
Law Center for Disability Rights, located at Loyola Law School in Los
Angeles. She founded the program to help low-income families work
with schools to obtain services for children with learning difficulties
and disabilities.

"She comes into the process with an open mind," says Wesley Par-
sons, a special education attorney for the Los Angeles Unified School
District [LAUSD] who has worked with Steel. "She focuses on resolv-
ing situations in a manner that's both beneficial to the child and practical. I think she has a good grasp on how to address the need of stu-

dents with learning disabilities in the best possible way and is willing to work with the district in meeting those needs."

Steel's goal: to make sure each child is properly assessed and receives the services and rights granted them by the law. The kind of support that keeps them in school and helps them find ways to succeed.

And she knows how difficult it can be to stay the course—long before she was a lawyer, she was a high school dropout with undiagnosed learning disabilities.

## An Impossible Dream?

National figures suggest that about 35%, twice the percentage of those without learning disabilities, drop out of high school. That statistic is why Steel is working with students such as 18-year-old Jason Artola, a sophomore at Verdugo Hills High School in Tujunga, California.

Although Artola has been tested as being of higher than average intelligence, until 2001, he knew only failure. Other students called him "stupid" or "retarded." They said his family must be stupid too.

One day in the cafeteria of his former school, a group of about five students swarmed around him, calling him names. They grabbed his backpack and scattered its contents on the floor. They pushed him against a wall, then laughed as they walked away.

Artola turned and saw the stares. He quickly gathered his things off the floor and left school. He took the bus to Griffith Park, and he started to run. He ran until his chest heaved and his mind cleared.

By the time he got home, however, the feelings of pain and frustration had returned. He went to his bedroom, closed the door and lay still on the bed. What would it be like to die, he asked himself. Which knife should he use?

Then he thought about his family and knew that wasn't the solution. Desperate to keep her son in school, Artola's mother contacted Steel after hearing about her through a co-worker. Steel studied the youth's background and met with school officials.

He began to see improvement in 2001, when he transferred to Verdugo Hills High School. He was assigned tutors, and other students took notes for him, allowing him to focus on what the teacher was saying. He was placed in regular classes rather than special education classes and for the first time received passing marks.

And for the first time, he was academically eligible to participate in athletics. He went out for cross country, soccer and track.

"I felt school pride for the first time in my life," Artola says. "The first time I wore a school uniform. . . . I teared up a little bit because it was what I wanted for so long. It was my dream to get into some sport."

He seemed to flourish, but then in April 2002, Artola received a report card with two failing marks. He was removed from the track team. He started missing classes. "It's hard to keep going," he now says. "I feel like giving up."

Gayle Glazer, inclusion facilitator at the school, says he has been switched to classes that will provide him with more individual attention. Notes will be taken for all his classes, not just one. And he will be given more time to work on assignments.

"We're doing everything we can to help him become successful," Glazer says. "It's frustrating because he's so bright. Now, it's a matter of how hard he's willing to work."

## An Arduous Journey

Steel knows about the frustrations and the hard work. She grew up dreaming of becoming a writer, but words, like all else, were a part of her chaos. In 1981, she dropped out of Hollywood High School and graduated from a continuing-education program. Her next six years were spent stumbling a few steps in many directions.

She lasted six weeks in welding school, one day in real estate school, an hour or so in a bartending program. She was a beautician for a while, but that didn't work out either. Nothing did. At the same time, she was trying to fill the voids in her life with drink, drugs and a vague notion that things would work out, just as they did in movies, her place of escape. The only time she could forget that her life was going nowhere was during long afternoons at the Fox, Egyptian, Vogue, Pacific [movie theaters]. She saw *Tommy* six times.

Eventually, she enrolled at Long Beach City College to study writing. For an English class, she was assigned an exercise in comparison and contrast, so she wrote about similarities and differences between health clubs and bars.

She says she worked hard but failed the assignment. Her professor could not understand her writing, but he had a daughter with dyslexia, and he recognized its symptoms in Steel's work. Tests confirmed she suffered from disabilities affecting her abilities to read and write.

"All the sudden, it wasn't me that was the problem," she says. "It was my brain that was the problem. I can't explain how much it relieved me. . . . Suddenly, I knew that I was going to be OK."

Steel began working with tutors and note-takers, utilizing books on tape and developing new strategies to process information. She would dictate papers instead of writing directly. She made time to get organized before setting out on a task—even something as simple as driving across town.

Steel graduated from Long Beach City College, where she served as student body president, and in 1993, she received a bachelor's degree in creative writing from San Francisco State. In 1999, 12 years after enrolling at Long Beach, she graduated from UCLA School of Law.

Throughout college, there were times, she says, when it seemed that all the information being fed into her brain might somehow abandon her as she struggled to live life in a new way, with new eyes and new hope.

What fueled her was the realization that ultimately she might be able to help others with learning disabilities.

"I got to law school, and a couple things happened," she says. "I took an educational law class, and I started investigating students in high school and junior high school who had learning disabilities, whether or not they were getting accommodations, and I found out that they weren't."

She also discovered that students from low-income families were at a disadvantage in that they could not afford private attorneys to guide them through the process of assessment and compliance with state and federal laws. Nor could they afford private tutors. The Learning Rights Project started out as an independent nonprofit, but in 2000, it was taken in by the Western Law Center for Disability Rights, which now funds it. Working out of a small office, and with the assistance of six law clerks, Steel now assists about 35 clients.

## From Chaos to Light

Steel believes students in special education will benefit as LAUSD moves toward greater inclusion. "We need to educate students the same way we live in our communities," she says. "We don't want segregation in our communities, so we need to educate in an environment with people learning differently, looking differently. We need to teach students to accept each other in schools as well as communities."

Statistics gathered by the National Center for Learning Disabilities indicate that there are 2.8 million students nationwide receiving special education services for learning disabilities. About 85% of them have difficulties in the area of reading. Of Los Angeles Unified School District's 736,675 students in kindergarten through 12th grade, 52,429 have been identified as having learning disabilities.

Learning disabilities and behavioral issues easily become entangled. More than three-quarters of incarcerated youths have learning disabilities, Steel estimates, and it was through the juvenile court system that she met Sandra, 16, a junior at Wilson High School.

She was kicked out of school in eighth grade and got in trouble with the law. After she realized she had to change her life, the question became how, and that's what Steel helped her understand.

"She told me that I was smart," Sandra says. "It's not that I'm not capable of doing things. It's just that l need more time to do stuff. I'm as capable as regular students. At first, I didn't believe her."

Over time, however, Steel proved to be right. Sandra's disability affected reading comprehension, written expression and math calculation. She was accommodated through tutors, books on tape, use of a computer for exams and assignments with software allowing her to check grammar and spelling. She also was given more time to complete exams.

This year, she is receiving straight A's.

## New Beginnings

As it is becoming for students like Artola and Sandra, life for Steel has been a series of new beginnings. She was married in 2002—she and her fiance, Mark Challed, a road foreman for Metrolink, headed to a Las Vegas chapel and tied the knot at a ceremony officiated by an Elvis impersonator. It is her second marriage. She doesn't like talking about the first.

Steel continues healing in many aspects of life. From time to time, she encounters ghosts of the past, familiar faces on the streets of Hollywood. "Literally, the people I hung around with, they're homeless, on the streets now. Some are dead or in jail."

When she sees them, she realizes how close she came. How far she came.

As she looks at the artwork hanging in her office and reflects on her life, she describes how the darkness becomes light in the upper left corner. "Chaos to light," says Steel. "It's always chaos to light."

# RICH MAN, POOR READER

Richard Lee Colvin

Millionaire stockbroker Charles Schwab realized he had dyslexia only when his own son was diagnosed with the learning disability, explains *Los Angeles Times* journalist Richard Lee Colvin. Growing up at a time before dyslexia was widely recognized, Schwab struggled with reading throughout his school days, Colvin relates. However, he did well in subjects such as math and science, graduated from Stanford University, and became extremely successful in the business world. After his son was diagnosed, Schwab became interested in reaching out to other parents who have children with learning disabilities. He established the Parents Educational Resource Center to help families learn about dyslexia and access school programs, as Colvin describes in the following article.

Charles Schwab, the millionaire discount stockbroker, doesn't read for pleasure. Never has. Never will.

For him, letters seem like abstract objects scattered across the page. If he were to read an unfamiliar text, such as a novel, or this story, it would take him so long to tease the letters into a recognizable pattern that the meaning of the phrase or the sentence would likely escape the first few times he labored through it.

Schwab has dyslexia, by far the most common of the learning disabilities related to spoken or written language. But, growing up, he didn't know he had a handicap. He only knew that he read terribly slowly and could barely write. Yet, he managed.

"I didn't ever think I was stupid," said the still boyishly handsome 58-year-old Schwab, who avoided the debilitating self-esteem problems experienced by many who have learning disabilities. "I'm real good at concepts and visualization. I get into a meeting with business associates and I can process all kinds of stuff and get to the conclusion much faster than other people who have to go step by step, processing things sequentially."

In school, he was outgoing, enabling him to befriend teachers, who were patient with him because they thought he had potential. He captained the golf team at his Santa Barbara, CA, high school and his sweet swing attracted the attention of the Stanford University golf coach. There, he flunked French and, twice, basic English. But he made up for it by doing well in quantitative and technical courses, such as math, economics and chemistry.

A lifetime of quietly and successfully coping, however, came to an end in the 1980s when Helen and Charles Schwab acted on their suspicions about their son's learning difficulties in fourth grade. His teachers, expressing a common and misguided view, tried to convince them that he was developing slowly but not abnormally and that he would eventually catch up. But they had him tested anyway and found that he was dyslexic and two grades behind in his reading level.

It was only then that the elder Schwab finally had a name for his own reading difficulties. "I had all the same issues when I was a kid going through school but they didn't have a name for it," he said. "You put two and two together and think, 'Wow, where did he get it?' It doesn't come through the water system."

Now, new research is confirming a genetic link.

## A Private Cause Goes Public

Schwab and his wife, Helen, try to preserve their son's privacy by not using his first name. He is currently a sophomore at a Southern California college and continues to have difficulty with his reading disability—as do about 3% of college students nationally.

The Schwabs are anything but private, however, when talking about the difficulty they had finding teachers and experts knowledgeable about their son's condition and arranging the help he needed. "It was a bewildering time," Helen Schwab recalled. "It's scary, when you think there's something that can be done for your child but you don't know what it is and there isn't one place for you to go to for help."

It took the Schwabs three years of tests, research, and meetings with teachers and other experts to find the school, tutors and related services their son needed. It was a frustrating process, even for a family as well-educated and well-off as they were. And it isn't over yet. Coping is still difficult at times.

But out of it came a desire to help other parents benefit from what they had learned. So, in 1987, the Schwabs set up the Parents Educational Resource Center in San Mateo, south of San Francisco. Operating on a $1 million annual budget from the Charles and Helen Schwab Foundation, the center helps 1,000 families a month learn about dyslexia and evaluate schools and the tutors and services the public schools are obligated to provide.

In 1995, the center began reaching out to parents beyond the immediate Bay Area by assembling "Bridges to Reading," a $20, user-friendly package of pamphlets, audiotapes and checklists that offers the latest information on dyslexia as well as practical, well-tested tips and strategies.

In March 1996, the center and the Schwab foundation unveiled the nation's first Resource Collection for Learning Differences in a public library at the new San Francisco Main Library. The collection includes audio- and videotapes, printed materials and an online database of information and referrals. Also available are voice-operated computers to make the library more accessible to the learning disabled.

Each of the projects is aimed at arming parents with information they need to be effective advocates for their children. "If a child is going to be successful, he or she needs a parent to really pave the road," Charles Schwab said.

## Long Journey to Success

Schwab's father was an assistant district attorney, his mother a home-maker. The Catholic schools he attended growing up near Chico, CA, before moving to Santa Barbara, emphasized drills and basic skills, the kind of instruction he needed.

At Stanford, he got by with the help of roommates and friends who took notes for him because he found it impossible to listen to a lecture and write down what was being said. He then attended Stanford's business school, which he said was easier for him than the general curriculum because it focused on subjects for which he knew the vocabulary.

After graduating in 1961, he and two associates started an investment advisory newsletter, which grew into a $20-million mutual fund. The company fell apart after the stock market tumbled in 1969.

Schwab, then $100,000 in debt, borrowed money from an uncle to start a stock brokerage that eventually became the San Francisco–based Charles Schwab Co. In 1975, the company began discounting its fee and took off. Schwab sold it in 1983 to raise expansion capital but bought it back four years later for $324 million in cash and securities. Six months later he took the company public in an offering that valued it at $100 million more than he paid for it.

His holdings in 1995 were valued at $825 million.

Schwab said he believed it was fortunate for him, in a way, that his disability was not identified until after he had achieved great success. "I just dealt with it," he said. "I worked extremely hard at things and I didn't understand what failure was about."

## Facing Competition

Now, however, the competition to get into top colleges is far more demanding. Classes are large and teachers have little time to give students special attention. And modern instructional techniques that downplay basic skills may make it more difficult for dyslexic students to learn.

When the problems of their son—the youngest of five children, three of whom are from Charles Schwab's first marriage—surfaced,

Helen Schwab panicked. Then she set about to find out what to do, which involved visits to specialists, doctors, testing experts and others.

"If you sense that your child has a problem, you have to go after it and try to ferret out the best answers," she said.

But that is not easily done. Although learning disabilities are common, they are poorly understood. A Roper national survey released in 1995 found that 80% of Americans associated learning disabilities with mental retardation although, in fact, there is no connection. Shockingly, the same survey found that 70% of teachers were similarly misinformed.

Another survey, by the National Institute of Child Health and Human Development, found that only 10% of the nation's teachers believe they know how to help children with learning disabilities. And teachers say they feel most inadequate when it comes to dealing with the severe reading problems, or dyslexia, that is manifest in more than 85% of learning disability cases.

In the past, it was thought that dyslexics had vision problems that caused them to see the mirror image of some letters or numbers. Now, however, dyslexia is defined broadly as the inability to identify words.

G. Reid Lyon, director of learning disabilities research at the National Institute of Child Health and Human Development, says dyslexics have trouble breaking words down into sounds.

"There is no quick fix to this," Lyon said. "Teaching children to read who have learning difficulties is extraordinarily difficult."

What seems to work best, he said, is "explicit, direct instruction in the sounds of our language and phonics," especially if it is begun in the first grade or even earlier.

Unfortunately, that type of instruction disappeared in many California classrooms in 1987, when the state introduced a new, literature-based approach to teaching reading.

## A Lifelong Issue

In 1995, a panel appointed by California Supt. of Public Instruction Delaine Eastin called for a return of so-called direct instruction. But that idea was met with resistance despite pressure from the Legislature and the state Board of Education.

Meanwhile, parents continue to be duped into buying one miracle cure or another. Alexa Culwell, the executive director of the Parents Educational Resource Center, said desperate parents are being taken advantage of by entrepreneurs selling hope in the form of shaking beds, colored eyeglass lenses, chiropractic treatments and regimens involving staring at flickering candles. None of those work.

"Parents have no idea that this is a lifelong issue," Culwell said.

Rather than seducing them with quick fixes, the center helps parents help their children develop a wide range of strategies, including alternatives to reading as a means of learning. For example, dyslexic students learn better if they develop their ability to listen carefully, ask questions, create explicit mental images of an idea and improve their memory by discussing or applying new information.

Lyon said the center's comprehensive approach "has been a god-send to parents and kids" because it gives them expertise that teachers and administrators often lack. "Hopefully the awareness will sift on through to the teacher preparation institutions."

# ORGANIZATIONS TO CONTACT

The editors have compiled the following list of organizations concerned with the issues presented in this book. The descriptions are derived from materials provided by the organizations. All have publications or information available for interested readers. The list was compiled on the date of publication of the present volume; the information provided here may change. Be aware that many organizations take several weeks or longer to respond to inquiries, so allow as much time as possible.

### American Speech-Language-Hearing Association (ASHA)
10801 Rockville Pike, Rockville, MD 20852
(800) 638-8255
e-mail: actioncenter@asha.org • website: www.asha.org

The mission of this professional, scientific, and credentialing association is to ensure that all people with speech, language, and hearing disorders have access to quality services to help them communicate more effectively. ASHA sponsors an annual convention, fosters innovative research and public awareness, and works to increase insurance coverage for communication disorders. Its many publications include the quarterly journal *Language, Speech, and Hearing Services in Schools* and the newsletter *ASHA Leader Online*.

### Attention Deficit Disorder Association (ADDA)
1788 Second St., Suite 200, Highland Park, IL 60035
(847) 432-ADDA • fax: (847) 432-5874
e-mail: mail@add.org • website: www.add.org

ADDA's mission is to help adults with attention deficit hyperactivity disorder (ADHD) lead happier, more successful lives through education, research, and public advocacy. The association holds conferences and regional workshops, sponsors research into ADHD's causes and treatment, and assists local support groups for adults with ADHD. It also works to educate professionals, legislators, the public, and the media about the realities of ADHD. The organization publishes the fact sheet "Guiding Principles for the Diagnosis and Treatment of Attention Deficit Hyperactivity Disorder" and the newsletter *FOCUS*.

### Attention Deficit Information Network (AD-IN)
58 Prince St., Needham, MA 02492
(781) 455-9895
e-mail: adin@gis.net • website: www.addinfonetwork.com

Through a network of regional chapters, AD-IN offers support and information to families of children with attention deficit disorder (ADD), adults with ADD, and professionals. AD-IN serves as a community resource for information on training programs and speakers for those who work with individuals with ADD. The organization also presents conferences and workshops for parents and professionals on current issues, research, and treatment for ADD. Among its publications are information packets, audiocassettes, and videotapes such as *What Comes Next? Life Skills and Transitioning to the Workplace for the Young Adult*.

## Children and Adults with Attention-Deficit/Hyperactivity Disorder (CHADD)
8181 Professional Place, Suite 150, Landover, MD 20785
(800) 233-4050 • (301) 306-7070 • fax: (301) 306-7090
e-mail: national@chadd.org • website: www.chadd.org

CHADD is dedicated to serving individuals with attention deficit hyperactivity disorder (ADHD) and to presenting an informed perspective on ADHD. Through collaborative leadership, advocacy, research, education, and support, CHADD provides science-based information about ADHD and related learning disorders to parents, educators, professionals, the media, and the general public. Its publications include fact sheets, the electronic newsletter *News from CHADD*, and the bimonthly magazine *Attention!*

## Council for Exceptional Children (CEC)
1110 N. Glebe Rd., Suite 300, Arlington, VA 22201
(703) 620-3660 • fax: (703) 264-9494
e-mail: service@cec.sped.org • website: www.cec.sped.org

The Council for Exceptional Children is the largest international professional organization dedicated to improving educational outcomes for individuals with exceptionalities, students with disabilities, and/or the gifted. CEC lobbies for appropriate governmental policies, sets professional standards, provides continual professional development, advocates for newly and historically underserved individuals with exceptionalities, and helps professionals obtain conditions and resources necessary for effective professional practice. The council's publications include the quarterly journal *Exceptional Children*, the bimonthly journal *Teaching Exceptional Children*, and the *CEC Today* newsletter.

## Council for Learning Disabilities (CLD)
PO Box 4014, Leesburg, VA 20177
(571) 258-1010 • fax: (571) 258-1011
website: www.cldinternational.org

This international organization is composed of professionals from diverse disciplines who are committed to enhancing the education and development of individuals with learning disabilities. CLD establishes standards of excellence in education and promotes innovative strategies for research, practice, and policy through interdisciplinary collaboration and advocacy. The council hosts an annual conference and sponsors local chapters. It publishes *Learning Disability Quarterly*, the bimonthly journal *Intervention in School and Clinic*, the bimonthly newsletter *LD Forum*, and several fact sheets.

## Dyslexia Awareness and Resource Center (DARC)
928 Carpinteria St., Suite 2, Santa Barbara, CA 93103
(805) 963-7339 • fax: (805) 963-6581
e-mail: info@dyslexia-center.com • website: www.dyslexiacenter.org

DARC is committed to raising public awareness about dyslexia and attention deficit disorder. The center conducts outreach and training seminars for public and private schools, the juvenile court systems, literacy programs, and other social service agencies. It also provides direct one-on-one services to individuals with dyslexia and attention deficit disorder. DARC sponsors an annual conference and maintains a resource library containing hundreds of books, audiocassettes, and videotapes about learning disabilities.

## International Dyslexia Association (IDA)
Chester Bldg., Suite 382, 8600 LaSalle Rd., Baltimore, MD 21286-2044
(800) 222-3123 • (410) 296-0232 • fax: (410) 321-5069
e-mail: info@interdys.org • website: www.interdys.org

The oldest learning disabilities organization in the United States, IDA focuses on the study and treatment of dyslexia. The association concentrates its resources in four major areas: information and referral services, scientific research, public policy and legal advocacy, and direct services to professionals in the field of learning disabilities. IDA hosts an annual international conference, and local chapters conduct seminars and support groups. The association is also developing programs designed to provide services such as testing, tutoring, and remedial instruction directly to individuals with dyslexia. IDA publishes the fact sheet "Dyslexia Basics," the quarterly newsletter *Perspectives*, and the yearly scholarly journal *Annals of Dyslexia*.

## Learning Disabilities Association of America (LDA)
4156 Library Rd., Pittsburgh, PA 15234-1349
(412) 341-1515 • fax: (412) 344-0224
e-mail: info@ldaamerica.org • website: www.ldanatl.org

Dedicated to identifying the causes and promoting effective treatment of learning disabilities, LDA encourages neurophysiological and psychological research and works to improve educational opportunities for students who have learning disabilities. The association also strives to protect the legal rights of individuals with learning disabilities and their families. LDA offers an information and referral network for persons with learning disabilities. It sponsors an annual international conference, and its state affiliates hold workshops, symposiums, and support groups. Among its publications are numerous pamphlets and position papers, the bimonthly newsletter *LDA Newsbriefs*, and the quarterly *Learning Disabilities: A Multidisciplinary Journal*.

## Learning Disabilities Association of Canada (LDAC)
323 Chapel St., Suite 200, Ottawa, Ontario, Canada K1N 7Z2
(613) 238-5721 • fax: (613) 235-5391
e-mail: information@ldac-taac.ca • website: www.ldac-taac.ca

LDAC strives to ensure that individuals with learning disabilities are provided with equitable opportunities to develop to their full potential. With chapters in each province of Canada, the association collects and disseminates information on learning disabilities, holds regional workshops and seminars, and hosts a biannual national conference. LDAC also works to influence public policy in areas affecting people with learning disabilities, including health, prevention, research, literacy, and education. It publishes a number of manuals, self-help books, and reference materials, including *Roadmap on Learning Disabilities for Employers* and *Destination Literacy: Identifying and Teaching Adults with Learning Disabilities*.

## National Association for Child Development (NACD)
549 25th St., Ogden, UT 84401-2422
(801) 621-8606 • fax: (801) 621-8389
e-mail: info@nacd.org • website: www.nacd.org

NACD specializes in learning problems caused by neurological inefficiencies, including learning disabilities and attention deficit disorder. The association conducts training programs for teachers and administrators that stress the neurological basis of learning. In addition, it operates an academy whose staff of therapists, educators, and developmentalists works with individual students and their families to overcome learning problems through the use of innovative techniques. NACD publishes the *Journal of the National Academy for Child Development* and provides informative articles on its website.

### National Association for the Education of African American Children with Learning Disabilities (NAEAACLD)
PO Box 09521, Columbus, OH 43209
(614) 237-6021 • fax: (614) 238-0929
e-mail: info@aacld.org
website: www.charityadvantage.com/aacld/HomePage.asp

This organization serves as an advocate for African American children with learning disabilities and their families. In particular, the association works to address the lack of cultural sensitivity in assessment and testing that has resulted in the disproportionate representation of African American children in special education. It acts as a clearinghouse of information on statistical and research data, effective assessment and testing, and model programming. NAEAACLD's publications include *One Child at a Time: A Parent Handbook and Resource Directory for African American Families with Children Who Learn Differently*, as well as the articles "Educating Kids Who Learn Differently," "Continued Mislabeling of African American Children Requires Parental Attention," and "The Law Ensures a 'Free Appropriate Public Education' for All."

### National Center for Learning Disabilities (NCLD)
381 Park Ave. South, Suite 1401, New York, NY 10016
(212) 545-7510 • (888) 575-7373 • fax: (212) 545-9665
website: www.ncld.org

In collaboration with scientific, educational, health, and literacy organizations, NCLD promotes research and develops programs that emphasize the early identification and treatment of learning disabilities and identify effective learning strategies. It helps to shape public policy by working closely with policy makers, federal agencies, and other national organizations to ensure that the specific needs of people with learning disabilities are fully considered in the development of national policies and legislation. In addition, the center strives to increase public awareness and understanding of learning disabilities through special campaigns. Its publications include the monthly *LD News: News You Can Use*, the report "Reading Comprehension Instruction for Students with Learning Disabilities," and several fact sheets, such as "Dyscalculia: A Quick Look," "Dyspraxia," "LD and the Arts," and "Being Your Own Advocate."

### National Information Center for Children and Youth with Disabilities (NICHCY)
PO Box 1492, Washington, DC 20013
(800) 695-0285 • fax: (202) 884-8441
e-mail: nichcy@aed.org • website: www.nichcy.org

NICHCY is an information and referral center on disabilities (including learning disabilities and attention deficit hyperactivity disorder) that serves the United States, Puerto Rico, and the U.S. territories. The center offers information on disability-related topics regarding children and young people. Trained information specialists are available to answer specific questions and to provide referrals to disability organizations, parent groups, and state agencies. NICHCY publishes a wide variety of material in English and Spanish, including the *News Digest* series, the fact sheet "Learning Disabilities," the briefing paper "Attention-Deficit/Hyperactivity Disorder," multimedia student guides, resource lists, and posters.

**Nonverbal Learning Disorders Association (NLDA)**
2446 Albany Ave., West Hartford, CT 06117
(860) 570-0217
e-mail: NLDA@nlda.org • website: www.nlda.org

NLDA is committed to facilitating education, research, and advocacy for children and adults who manifest disabilities associated with the syndrome of nonverbal learning disorders. The NLDA volunteer workforce includes individuals with learning disabilities, their families and associates, and those who provide professional care and intervention. The association works to fulfill its mission through lecture series, conferences, and the publication of both scholarly and informational material designed to broaden public awareness about nonverbal learning disorders. In addition, it sponsors a national network of support groups. Among NLDA's publications are *The NLDA Notebook* and the quarterly newsletter *NLD News*.

**Schwab Learning**
1650 S. Amphlett Blvd., Suite 300, San Mateo, CA 94402
(650) 655-2410 • fax: (650) 655-2411
website: www.schwablearning.org

Schwab Learning, an operating program of the Charles and Helen Schwab Foundation, focuses on helping children who have learning disabilities, attention deficit hyperactivity disorder, or other learning differences. The organization provides services that address the emotional, social, practical, and academic needs and concerns of children with learning difficulties and their parents. It sponsors conferences and seminars nationwide, as well as workshops specifically tailored to parents. Schwab Learning's publications include a weekly e-mail newsletter, press releases, fact sheets, booklets, the report "Navigating the LD Journey: A Study on the Experiences and Needs of Mothers of Children with Learning Differences," and the workbook *A Parent's Guide to Difficulties and Disabilities in Learning*.

# BIBLIOGRAPHY

## Books

Daniel G. Amen — *Healing ADD: The Breakthrough Program That Allows You to See and Heal the Six Types of Attention Deficit Disorder*. New York: G.P. Putnam's Sons, 2001.

William N. Bender — *Differentiating Instruction for Students with Learning Disabilities: Best Teaching Practices for General and Special Educators*. Thousand Oaks, CA: Corwin Press, 2002.

Dale S. Brown — *Learning a Living: A Guide to Planning Your Career and Finding a Job for People with Learning Disabilities, Attention Deficit Disorder, and Dyslexia*. Bethesda, MD: Woodbine House, 2000.

Maria Chivers — *Practical Strategies for Living with Dyslexia*. Philadelphia, PA: Jessica Kingsley, 2001.

Joyanne Cobb — *Learning How to Learn: Getting Into and Surviving College When You Have a Learning Disability*. Washington, DC: Child and Family Press, 2003.

Veronica Crawford — *Embracing the Monster: Overcoming the Challenges of Hidden Disabilities*. Baltimore, MD: Paul H. Brookes, 2001.

Wendy Sand Eckel — *Educating Tigers*. Baltimore, MD: PublishAmerica, 2000.

Anne Ford — *Laughing Allegra: The Inspiring Story of a Mother's Struggle and Triumph Raising a Daughter with Learning Disabilities*. New York: Newmarket Press, 2003.

Robert Frank — *The Secret Life of the Dyslexic Child: How She Thinks, How He Feels, How They Can Succeed*. Emmaus, PA: Rodale Press, 2002.

Lawrence J. Greene — *Roadblocks to Learning: Understanding the Obstacles That Can Sabotage Your Child's Academic Success*. New York: Warner Books, 2002.

Thom Hartmann — *ADHD Secrets of Success*. New York: SelectBooks, 2002.

Craig Hovey — *The ADD Hoax: Protect Your Child from the False Diagnosis That Is Threatening a Generation*. Roseville, CA: Prima, 2003.

Eric Jensen — *Different Brains, Different Learners: How to Reach the Hard to Reach*. San Diego, CA: Brain Store, 2000.

Amanda Kirby — *Dyspraxia: The Hidden Handicap*. London: Souvenir Press, 1999.

Rob Langston — *For the Children: Redefining Success in School and Success in Life*. Austin, TX: Turnkey Press, 2002.

Mel Levine — *A Mind at a Time*. New York: Simon & Schuster, 2002.

Christine Macintyre        *Dyspraxia 5–11: A Practical Guide*. London: David
                           Fulton, 2001.

J. Gordon Millichap        *Attention Deficit Hyperactivity and Learning Disorders:
                           Questions and Answers*. Chicago: PNB, 1998.

Esther Minskoff            *Academic Success Strategies for Adolescents with Learning
and David Allsopp          Disabilities and ADHD*. Baltimore, MD: Paul H.
                           Brookes, 2003.

Jonathan Mooney            *Learning Outside the Lines: Two Ivy League Students with
and David Cole             Learning Disabilities and ADHD Give You the Tools for
                           Academic Success and Educational Revolution*. New York:
                           Simon & Schuster, 2000.

Myrna Orenstein            *Smart but Stuck: Emotional Aspects of Learning
                           Disabilities and Imprisoned Intelligence*. Binghamton,
                           NY: Haworth Press, 2001.

Penny Hutchins             *Learning Disabilities: The Ultimate Teen Guide*. Lanham,
Paquette and Cheryl        MD: Scarecrow Press, 2002.
Gerson Tuttle

Kay Marie Porterfield      *Straight Talk About Learning Disabilities*. New York:
                           Facts On File, 1999.

Madeleine Portwood         *Understanding Developmental Dyspraxia*. London: David
                           Fulton, 2000.

Pano Rodis, Andrew         *Learning Disabilities and Life Stories*. Boston, MA: Allyn
Garrod, and Mary           & Bacon, 2001.
Lynn Boscardin, eds.

Arlyn J. Roffman           *Meeting the Challenge of Learning Disabilities in
                           Adulthood*. Baltimore, MD: Paul H. Brookes, 2000.

Bruce Roseman              *A Kid Just Like Me: A Father and Son Overcome the
                           Challenges of ADD and Learning Disabilities*. New York:
                           Perigee, 2001.

Mark Selikowitz            *Dyslexia and Other Learning Difficulties: The Facts*. New
                           York: Oxford University Press, 1998.

Sally Shaywitz             *Overcoming Dyslexia: A New and Complete Science-Based
                           Program for Reading Problems at Any Level*. New York:
                           Knopf, 2003.

Larry B. Silver            *The Misunderstood Child: Understanding and Coping with
                           Your Child's Learning Disabilities*. New York: Times
                           Books, 1998.

Corinne Smith and          *Learning Disabilities: A to Z*. New York: Simon &
Lisa Strick                Schuster, 1999.

Robert J. Sternberg and    *Our Labeled Children: What Every Parent and Teacher
Elena L. Grigorenko        Needs to Know About Learning Disabilities*. Reading,
                           MA: Perseus Books, 1999.

Rhonda Stone               *The Light Barrier: A Color Solution to Your Child's Light-
                           Based Reading Difficulties*. New York: St. Martin's Press,
                           2002.

| B. Jacqueline Stordy and Malcolm J. Nicholl | *The LCP Solution: The Remarkable Nutritional Treatment for ADHD, Dyslexia, and Dyspraxia*. New York: Ballantine Books, 2000. |
| Harry Sylvester | *Legacy of the Blue Heron: Living with Learning Disabilities*. Farmington, ME: Oxton House, 2002. |
| Rondalyn Varney Whitney | *Bridging the Gap: Raising a Child with Nonverbal Learning Disorder*. New York: Perigee, 2002. |
| Bernice Y.L. Wong, ed. | *Learning About Learning Disabilities*. San Diego, CA: Academic Press, 1998. |

## Periodicals

| Stephen J. Cannell | "How to Spell Success," *Reader's Digest*, August 2000. |
| Christina Cheakalos et al. | "Heavy Mettle," *People*, October 30, 2000. |
| Christine Gorman | "The New Science of Dyslexia," *Time*, July 28, 2003. |
| Jane Gross | "Paying for a Disability Diagnosis to Gain Time on College Boards," *New York Times*, September 26, 2002. |
| D'Arcy Jenish | "Reclaiming the Good Life," *Maclean's*, May 15, 2000. |
| Barbara Kantrowitz and Anne Underwood | "Dyslexia and the New Science of Reading," *Newsweek*, November 22, 1999. |
| Willow Lawson | "Lost Boys: Common Cause for Learning Disabilities Overlooked," *Psychology Today*, March/April 2003. |
| Mary Lord | "Not Just Kid Stuff Anymore," *U.S. News & World Report*, February 21, 2000. |
| David L. Marcus | "One Class, and 20 Learning Styles," *U.S. News & World Report*, April 9, 2001. |
| Ann Marsh | "When the Alphabet Is a Struggle," *Forbes*, September 6, 1999. |
| Robert McGough | "Scans of Kids' Brains at Work May Shed Light on Disabilities," *Wall Street Journal*, May 24, 2002. |
| Annetta Miller | "Hot Topic: LD Labeling," *Working Mother*, May 2003. |
| Betsy Morris | "Overcoming Dyslexia," *Fortune*, May 13, 2002. |
| Christine Mullis | "Faking It: Using Learning Disabilities to Boost SAT Scores," *Psychology Today*, January/February 2003. |
| John O'Neil | "Finding the Right College, and Getting In," *New York Times*, April 13, 2003. |
| Romesh Ratnesar | "Lost in the Middle," *Time*, September 14, 1998. |
| Craig Savoye | "Bringing Literacy Home for Adult Learners," *Christian Science Monitor*, September 11, 2001. |
| Robert Sheppard | "Why Kids Can't Read: As Science Cracks the Code, Parents Fight for Their Children's Right to Specialized Education," *Maclean's*, September 7, 1998. |

Lisa Snell

"Special Education Confidential: How Schools Use the 'Learning Disability' Label to Cover Up Their Failures," *Reason*, December 2002.

Sheila Sobell

"How to Spot a Learning Disability," *Woman's Day*, September 1, 2000.

Marianne Szegedy-Maszak

"The Mind Maze: Can 'Distraction' Be Found in the Brain's Biochemistry?" *U.S. News & World Report*, May 6, 2002.

# INDEX

Rourke, Byron, 37

schemas, 106–107
school
　environment, 34–35
　involvement of parents in, 54
　problems, effect of, on family,
　　120–32
*Schooled Society, The* (Dewey), 104
Schwab, Charles, 141–45
selective attention, 18
self-acceptance, 118
self-esteem, 35, 65, 93, 129–30
self-image
　of people with learning disabilities,
　　10–11
　positive refraining of, 65
self-perception, 35
self-regulation, 19
services, for students with learning
　disabilities, 136–40
Shapiro, Joan, 29
Shaywitz, Sally E., 23–24
Siegel, Linda, 37
Skinner, B.F., 37
Smith, Sally L., 10, 98
Sousa, David A., 83
Spalding, Romalda, 37
special education, 114–19
special education teachers, 47, 79–81
spelling problems, 16–17
spinal cord, 30
Steel, Janeen, 136–40
Stillman, Bessie, 37
Stovsky, Renee, 133
Stowe, Cynthia M., 20
Strategies Integration Model (SIM),
　87, 88–91
Strauss, Alfred, 32–33
strengths, focusing on, 110–11
strephosymbolia, 32, 36–37
stress, 35
students
　arts instruction for learning-
　　disabled, 98–108
　college, with learning disabilities,
　　55–60

gaining access to services for
　learning-disabled, 136–40
harmful effects of labeling, 109–12
learning strategies for learning-
　disabled, 83–91
Sturomski, Neil, 84, 86
substance abuse, 94

teacher preparation, 76–82
teachers
　collaboration by, 78
　competencies for, 77–82
　general education and, 77–79
　identification of learning disability
　　by, 44
　labeling by, 111
　misconceptions about students
　　made by, 98–99
　special education and, 47, 79–81
teaching methods
　nonstandard, 47–48
　reading, 37, 40
　*see also* learning strategies
television watching, 51
testing, 45–46
therapists, 66–67
therapy, speech and language, 47
time sense, 101
treatment, 37–38

universities. *See* colleges and
　universities

vocational rehabilitation agencies,
　49
Vygotsky, Lev, 104

Waldorf education, 131–32
Werner, Heinz, 32–33
West, Thomas G., 26–27
Whole Language reading approach,
　40
Winkler, Henry, 11
workplace issues. *See* employment
　issues
writing disorders, 16–17